MAKING HISTORY
ESSAYS ON THE *FORNALDARSÖGUR*

EDITED BY

MARTIN ARNOLD AND ALISON FINLAY

VIKING SOCIETY FOR NORTHERN RESEARCH
UNIVERSITY COLLEGE LONDON
2010

© Viking Society for Northern Research 2010

Printed by Short Run Press Limited, Exeter

ISBN: 978-0-903521-84-0

The printing of this book is made possible by a gift to the University of Cambridge in memory of Dorothea Coke, Skjaeret, 1951.

Front cover: The Levisham Slab. Late tenth- or early eleventh-century Viking grave cover, North Yorkshire. © Corpus of Anglo-Saxon Stone Sculpture, University of Durham. Photographer J. T. Lang. The editors are grateful to Levisham Local History Society for their help and support.

CONTENTS

Introduction
RORY McTURK v

Sǫgubrot af fornkonungum: Mythologised History for Late
Thirteenth-Century Iceland
ELIZABETH ASHMAN ROWE 1

Hrólfs saga kraka and the Legend of Lejre
TOM SHIPPEY 17

Enter the Dragon. Legendary Saga Courage and the Birth of
the Hero
ÁRMANN JAKOBSSON 33

Þóra and Áslaug in Ragnars saga loðbrókar. Women, Dragons
and Destiny
CAROLYNE LARRINGTON 53

Hyggin ok forsjál. Wisdom and Women's Counsel in Hrólfs
saga Gautrekssonar
JÓHANNA KATRÍN FRIÐRIKSDÓTTIR 69

Við þik sættumsk ek aldri. Ǫrvar-Odds saga and the Meanings
of Ǫgmundr Eyþjófsbani
MARTIN ARNOLD 85

The Tale of Hogni And Hedinn
TRANSLATED BY WILLIAM MORRIS AND EIRÍKR MAGNÚSSON
INTRODUCTION BY CARL PHELPSTEAD 105

The Saga of Ásmundr, Killer of Champions
TRANSLATED BY ALISON FINLAY 119

INTRODUCTION

RORY McTURK

There has recently been a welcome revival of interest in the *fornaldarsögur*, that group of Icelandic sagas known variously in English as 'mythical-heroic sagas', 'legendary sagas', 'sagas of times past', and 'sagas of Icelandic prehistory'. Gwyn Jones indicated the need for such a revival, for English readers at least, in 1961, finding that these sagas had been 'neglected not so much by choice as for lack of opportunity by the English reader'.[1] This presumably meant that at that time there were not enough translations or introductory accounts of them in English. This situation is now largely remedied. A bibliography of manuscripts, editions and translations of these sagas, and of secondary literature relating to them, is currently being compiled, under the title *Fornaldarsögur norðurlanda*, by M. J. Driscoll and Silvia Hufnagel, and is accessible on the Internet in an advanced state of preparation. The revival of critical and scholarly interest in these sagas, heralded at book length by Hermann Pálsson and Paul Edwards in 1971,[2] and by Stephen Mitchell twenty years later,[3] is now in full swing. Two collections of essays—not all of them in English, it is true—based on *fornaldarsaga* conferences held in Uppsala and Copenhagen and edited by the Icelandic-Swedish-Danish team that organised both conferences, appeared in 2003[4] and 2009[5] respectively, and that same team, having organised yet another such conference last year in Reykjavík, is currently preparing its proceedings for publication. The present volume arises out of the Viking Society Student Conference organised by Martin Arnold and hosted by the University of Hull's Andrew Marvell Centre on 28 February 2009. An indication of its contents may be given here.

[1] Gwyn Jones, trans., 1961. *Eirik the Red and other Icelandic sagas*, xv.
[2] Hermann Pálsson and Paul Edwards 1971. *Legendary fiction in medieval Iceland*, Studia Islandica 30.
[3] Stephen A. Mitchell 1991. *Heroic sagas and ballads*.
[4] Ármann Jakobsson, Annette Lassen and Agneta Ney, eds, 2003. *Fornaldarsagornas struktur och ideologi. Handlingar från ett symposium i Uppsala 31.8–2.9 2001*. Nordiska texter och undersökningar 28.
[5] Agneta Ney, Ármann Jakobsson and Annette Lassen, eds, 2009. *Fornaldarsagaerne: myter og virkelighed. Studier i de oldislandske fornaldarsögur Norðurlanda*.

Comparing Saxo's account (in Book VIII of his *Gesta Danorum*) of the legendary battle of Brávellir with the account of the same battle in the late thirteenth-century Icelandic *Sǫgubrot af fornkonungum*, Elizabeth Ashman Rowe argues that in the latter account the minimisation of Óðinn's role in the battle itself is due not to rationalisation—since the pre-battle generation here shows marked Odinic features—but rather to a wish by the author to present the Danish king Haraldr hilditǫnn, leader of one of the battle's two warring parties, as a kind of pre-Christian martyr, and to suggest parallels between him and the Norwegian kings Haraldr hárfagri and Óláfr Tryggvason. Tom Shippey gives a straightforward analysis of the structure of *Hrólfs saga kraka*, explaining its inconsistencies and superfluities in terms of its author's evident wish to include everything he knows, however remotely relevant. Shippey further summarises the other medieval Scandinavian accounts of this saga's eponymous but for the most part purely formal hero, showing the ways in which they contradict and agree with each other. He compares in passing King Hrólfr with King Arthur and finds *Hrólfs saga kraka* comparable to *Vǫlsunga saga*, both in its inclusiveness and, as he suggests, in its ultimate historicity—though this, he admits, is less easy to confirm than in the case of *Vǫlsunga saga*. Ármann Jakobsson, referring mainly to the dragon fights of Sigurðr Fáfnisbani and Ragnarr loðbrók, in *Vǫlsunga saga* and *Ragnars saga* respectively, sees the dragon in medieval tradition as symbolic of the fear which young people in particular are best equipped to conquer—hence the greater success of Sigurðr and Ragnarr in fighting dragons than that of Beowulf. At the same time the dragon, in giving birth to a hero through its death, becomes a parental figure as well as an emblem of teenage power. Carolyne Larrington concentrates on *Ragnars saga*, showing that Ragnarr's slaying of a serpentine dragon in order to win his first wife Þóra is a rite of passage for her as much as for him, and that the snake-like birthmark in the eye of his son Sigurðr by his second wife, Áslaug, is a pointer to Ragnarr's relative inferiority as a hero, since only when he sees this mark on his newborn son does Ragnarr deign to acknowledge Áslaug as the daughter of Sigurðr Fáfnisbani. Larrington's discussion includes a comparison of Áslaug with the Mélusine figure of French legend, another woman with serpentine connections, and an analysis of some of the verses of *Ragnars saga*. Jóhanna Katrín Friðriksdóttir shows how *Hrólfs saga Gautrekssonar* gives the lie to the proverbial statement, found not in this saga but not infrequently elsewhere, that 'cold are the counsels of women'. This saga, she argues, under the four headings of foresight, loyalty, caution and hospitality, imparts wisdom to its audience by conveying it through female characters juxtaposed with less than wise males, and does so in terms that are applicable generally as well as to the saga's specific concerns, somewhat in the manner of *Hávamál*. Martin Arnold makes use of textual criticism and modern literary theory in showing how Qgmundr Eyþjófsbani, a mysterious, loose-end figure in the older redactions of *Qrvar-Odds saga*, becomes in the younger redactions not so much an *alter ego* of Qrvar-Oddr, or a figure of death, as a personification and reminder of the fate prophesied for him by the sybil at the beginning of the saga. Carl Phelpstead reprints and introduces, as a tribute to William Morris and Eiríkr Magnússon, their translation, published in 1875, of the story now known as *Sǫrla þáttr* but entitled in their translation, hardly less appropriately, 'The Tale of Hogni and Hedinn'. In this tale, established as part of the *fornaldarsaga* canon in C. C. Rafn's three-volume edition of 1829–30, the hero Sǫrli functions as little more than a bridge between the story of the theft of Freyja's necklace or collar (referred to elsewhere as the *Brísingamen*) and that of the potentially everlasting fight between Hǫgni and Heðinn. The language of the Morris-Magnússon translation, Phelpstead finds, is not so much archaic as Icelandicised. Alison Finlay, finally, produces and introduces her own translation of *Ásmundar saga kappabana*, showing in her Introduction that this story of a fight to the death between two half-brothers, closely paralleled in Book VII of Saxo's *Gesta Danorum* and relying heavily on poems of eddic type, versions of which were also known to Saxo, betrays only the faintest recollection of the tragic story of a fight between father and son which forms the subject of the Old High German *Hildebrandslied*, to which it is more distantly related.

The present volume is thus fully in line with current trends in saga research and an essential supplement to the Uppsala, Copenhagen and Reykjavík volumes. There is a great deal more in it than this Introduction has revealed, as readers are hereby invited to find out for themselves. In John Gower's terms, it contains both 'lust' and 'lore' in more or less equal measure, whether one is thinking of its articles or its translations.

SǪGUBROT AF FORNKONUNGUM: MYTHOLOGISED HISTORY FOR LATE THIRTEENTH-CENTURY ICELAND

ELIZABETH ASHMAN ROWE

Introduction

The battle of Brávellir is one of the most famous battles of legendary Scandinavia, but its current use in Old Norse studies is as evidence of Óðinn's fickle nature: after favouring the Danish king Haraldr hilditǫnn all his life, Óðinn withdraws his help when Haraldr is an old man on the battlefield and gives the victory to the Danes' enemy by teaching them a special military formation that previously he had taught only to Haraldr. In medieval Scandinavia, however, the battle of Brávellir had an important place in historiography. Saxo Grammaticus makes it the centre of his plan for Book VIII of the *Gesta Danorum*, which draws on various aspects of the myth of Ragnarǫk. Moreover, the names of men and women who appear in the first ten books of the history reappear among the combatants at Brávellir, so that Saxo is in effect superimposing the great battle of Ragnarǫk upon ordinary chronology and making the battle at Brávellir the historical turning point when paganism is ended and Christianity introduced (Skovgaard-Petersen 1993, 57a). A different story of the battle was produced in late thirteenth-century Iceland and is preserved in a fragment now known as *Sǫgubrot af fornkonungum*.[1] As Skovgaard-Petersen observes, there are two notable differences between this work and Saxo's version (Skovgaard-Petersen 1987, 260–61; 1993, 57a). One is that the Icelanders whom Saxo places at the battle have been removed, presumably because the battle takes place long before the settlement of Iceland. The other is that Óðinn's role has been minimised, which Skovgaard-Petersen suggests is due to 'rationalism'. I would argue that even though Óðinn's role has indeed been minimised, the saga author's addition of a number of new mythological allusions would indicate that 'rationalism' cannot be the explanation.

---

[1] Bjarni Guðnason (1982, xl) argues that *Sǫgubrot* cannot have been composed earlier than the middle of the thirteenth century, and Wolf (1993, 597b) puts the *terminus post quem* of composition in the latter part of the thirteenth century. The *terminus ante quem* is provided by the manuscript fragment (AM 1 e ß 1 fol), which has been dated to around 1300 (Bjarni Guðnason 1982, xxxvi; Degnbol et al. 1989, 432).

Both Saxo and the Icelandic author are drawing on a now-lost *_Brávallaþula_ 'Metrical Name List of Brávellir' (Skovgaard-Petersen 1993, 56b). Saxo enumerates some 160 champions, often adding their nicknames and places of origin, and the Icelandic author gives a shorter version of the same list. Debate concerning the origin of the list has been prolonged and marked by nationalist bias from Norwegian scholars (e.g. Olrik 1894, 260–62; Olrik 1919, 182; Seip 1927; Hald 1975). However, Bjarni Guðnason (1958) offers a convincing case for twelfth-century Icelandic composition, and Stefán Karlsson (1975) discredits the linguistic arguments for an origin in southern Norway.

Once the Icelandic saga author had extracted an account of the battle from the _þula_ (Bjarni Guðnason 1982, xli), he set it into a larger historical narrative whose sources are likewise not fully understood. This narrative, which was widely known in medieval Iceland, tells how a kind of 'Viking empire' was established in ancient times. For example, Snorri Sturluson gives a version of the story in ch. 41 of _Ynglinga saga_ when he attributes the founding of the empire to Ívarr víðfaðmi of Sweden (_Heimskringla_, I 72):

> Ívarr víðfaðmi lagði undir sik allt Svíaveldi. Hann eignaðisk ok allt Danaveldi ok mikinn hlut Saxlands ok allt Austrríki ok inn fimmta hlut Englands.[2] Af hans ætt eru komnir Danakonungar ok Svíakonungar, þeir er þar hafa einvald haft.
>
> Ívarr Wide-Reacher made all Sweden subject to him. He also came to possess all Denmark and a great part of Saxony and all the Baltic and one-fifth of England. From his line are come those kings of the Danes and those kings of the Swedes who have had sole rule there.

Snorri probably obtained this information from _Skjǫldunga saga_, which was the source for much else in _Ynglinga saga_ (Bjarni Aðalbjarnarson 1979, xxxi–liv). _Skjǫldunga saga_ is now lost, but the sixteenth-century _Rerum Danicarum Fragmenta_, compiled in Latin by Arngrímur Jónsson, preserves a version of it (Bjarni Guðnason 1982, lxvi–lxx). Arngrímur's work has a lacuna at this point, so the absence of this passage there does not necessarily mean that it was also absent from the original _Skjǫldunga saga_. The fact that _Rerum Danicarum Fragmenta_ does say that Ívarr was the ruler of Sweden and Denmark, which is part of what Snorri relates, adds to the likelihood that _Skjǫldunga saga_ was Snorri's source here.

If _Skjǫldunga saga_ was the first to contain this story, the time-frame for the creation of the myth of the Viking empire would have been

---

[2] Presumably this refers to Northumbria; see ch. 3 of _Hákonar saga góða_, in which Snorri says _Norðimbraland er kallat fimmtungr Englands_ 'Northumbria is called a fifth of England' (_Heimskringla_, I 152–53).

between 1180 and 1220.³ The next text after *Ynglinga saga* to use this material is *Ágrip af sǫgu Danakonunga*, written sometime between 1261 and 1287, but it too does not name a source. In *Sǫgubrot af fornkonungum*, which cannot be dated very precisely but which might be a bit younger than *Ágrip*, we see a change in the story: the origin of the Viking empire has been pushed back in time, with its founder now said to be not Ívarr víðfaðmi but his father Hálfdan snjalli Haraldsson.⁴ Despite this change, *Skjǫldunga saga* seems to have been the ultimate source of *Sǫgubrot*'s history.⁵ The U redaction of *Hervarar saga ok Heiðreks*, which is dated to the early fourteenth century (Pritsak 1993, 283b), also includes the story of the Viking empire, but as it cites *konga sogum* 'kings' sagas' (Jón Helgason 1924, 156) as its source, presumably the redactor of this version was not the originator of the Viking-empire material.

The genealogy of Haraldr hilditǫnn

The question of origins is clearer when it comes to the genealogy of Haraldr hilditǫnn and his relation to his opponent at the battle of Brávellir. This man is named Hringr, and by the time *Sǫgubrot* was composed, Hringr was thought to be the same person as Sigurðr hringr, the father of Ragnarr loðbrók.⁶ In any case, Haraldr and Hringr were closely related, both being descended from Auðr, the daughter of Ívarr víðfaðmi. Auðr was Haraldr hilditǫnn's mother, and his father was her first husband, Hrœrekr slǫngvanbaugi of Denmark. Auðr's second husband was King Ráðbarðr of Holmgarðr. They had a son named Randvér, who was thus Haraldr's younger half-brother. Randvér's son was Hringr, who was thus Haraldr's half-nephew. The source for most of this is *Hyndluljóð* (st. 28), which some hold to have been composed in the tenth century (Nordal 1944, xxiv)

---

³ Wolf (1993, 597b) argues that Bjarni Aðalsteinsson's argument for a date of around 1180 for the composition of *Skjǫldunga saga* are weak, but because the saga is a source for Snorri's *Edda*, it has to be earlier than around 1220.

⁴ In a description of Ragnarr loðbrók, *Skjǫldunga saga* (75) specifies that he is third in line from Ívarr, meaning that Haraldr hilditǫnn was the first ruler of these countries after Ívarr, Sigurðr hringr was the second and Ragnarr was the third. The fact that this early text reckons the succession from Ívarr rather than from Hálfdan suggests that Ívarr was the founder of the Viking empire in the earliest version of the myth.

⁵ Repetitions in the narrative of *Sǫgubrot* lead Bjarni Guðnason (1982, xxxviii) to surmise that *Sǫgubrot* was compiled from two exemplars of *Skjǫldunga saga*.

⁶ Hringr is named as Ragnarr's father in ch. 6 of *Sǫgubrot* (59).

and others hold to have been a product of the twelfth century (Hollander 1962, 137; Turville-Petre 1964, 129):[7]

> Haraldr hilditǫnn, borinn Hrœreki,
> slǫngvanbauga, sonr var hann Auðar,
> Auðr diúpauðga Ívars dóttir,
> enn Ráðbarðr var Randvés faðir;
> þeir vóro gumnar goðom signaðir;
> alt er þat ætt þin, Óttarr heimsci.
> (*Edda*, 292–03)

> Haraldr War-tooth, born to Hrœrekr
> Slinger of rings, he was the son of Auðr,
> Auðr the Subtle, daughter of Ívarr,
> But Ráðbarðr was the father of Randvér;
> They were warriors dedicated to gods;
> All that is your family, foolish Óttarr.

Going back to Ívarr, then, it appears that, because he has no sons, his empire dissolves upon his death. Young Haraldr is being brought up in Russia by his mother and stepfather, and when Ráðbarðr learns of Ívarr's death, he sends Haraldr back to Denmark, where he becomes king, and from there he sets about regaining the kingdoms that his maternal grandfather had possessed.

It is worth noting that Saxo (Book VII) puts together a complete different ancestry for Haraldr hilditǫnn: his mother is Gurith (daughter of Alf Sigarsson of Sweden), and his father is Haldan Drotsson of Denmark. Earlier in Book VII, Saxo had stated that Haraldr was the son of Borkar and Gro, so either this was a slip, or there was more than one tradition about his parentage (Ellis Davidson and Fisher 1979–80, 119, n. 100). Possibly *Brávallaþula* had a reference to Haraldr's mother protecting him after a battle, for both Saxo and the Icelandic saga author have an episode in which this happens. In the *Gesta Danorum*, Gurith carries Haraldr away from a battlefield, at which point Haraldr is humiliatingly shot in the posterior by a distant archer. In *Sǫgubrot*, Auðr similarly protects her young son Haraldr by taking him away with her after the killing of her husband, but there is no reference to a shameful wound dealt from behind.

Is the account in Sǫgubrot rationalised?

Let us now turn to the question of whether the legendary history in *Sǫgubrot* is rationalised. The only reason for thinking so is its reduction of Óðinn's role in the battle of Brávellir. According to Saxo, Óðinn

---

[7] See Rowe (2005, 301–08) for a discussion of the problem.

impersonates Haraldr's servant Brúni and sows strife between Haraldr and Sigurðr. Haraldr is at this point blind from age but still able to fight, and the two armies meet at Brávellir. After multitudes are slain on both sides, Haraldr learns that the Swedish army is deployed in a boar's-snout formation like his own. Only Óðinn could have taught them this, and Haraldr realises that the god has turned against him. Brúni (that is, Óðinn) has been serving as Haraldr's charioteer, and because Haraldr is invulnerable to cuts from iron weapons, Brúni batters the king to death with his own club. *Sǫgubrot*, however, does not mention any divine intervention in the battle. Haraldr is killed by Brúni, but the latter is nowhere explicitly identified with Óðinn; he is simply described as a *hǫfðingi* 'chieftain' and *allra þeira manna vitrastr, er með honum váru* 'the wisest of all the men who were with him' (61), whom Haraldr appoints as his general. Presumably the saga author and his audience would have known that Brúni was Óðinn in disguise, but the text omits this information. An additional piece of evidence for rationalisation is the reason for Haraldr's invulnerability. Saxo presumably gives the original version of the myth when he says that Óðinn granted special protection to his protégé, just as he gave him a special ability to attack by teaching him the boar's-snout formation. *Sǫgubrot*, in contrast, says that Haraldr was invulnerable to iron because his people brought about his protection through *seið miklum* 'a great act of sorcery' (56). If these were the only changes related to mythology that the saga author makes, then it would be perfectly reasonable to describe *Sǫgubrot* as rationalised, but in fact the saga author includes two episodes before the battle that go a long way toward restoring Óðinn's place in this history.

In the first Odinic episode (50–52), Ívarr víðfaðmi maliciously stirs up trouble between Hrœrekr and his brother Helgi by telling him that everyone says that Haraldr is Helgi's child, not his, and that Hrœrekr ought to give his wife to Helgi outright if he is not going to take vengeance. Hrœrekr holds a tournament to welcome his brother back from his raiding, but where the other riders have lances, Hrœrekr equips himself with helmet and byrnie and sword and spear, and when Helgi comes at him with a lance, Hrœrekr runs him through with a spear—clearly an Odinic moment. Ívarr then returns to Denmark, and far from praising Hrœrekr for taking revenge, he calls the slaying *níðingsverk mikit* 'a very dishonourable deed' (52) and says that he will avenge his friend Helgi. Ívarr kills Hrœrekr and takes over his realm, so that he now rules Denmark as well as Sweden.

In the second Odinic episode (53–55), the historical characters are linked to the pagan gods. Having dreamed that a dragon (his fetch) disappears in a terrible storm and all his ships have been blown out of their safe harbour,

Ívarr summons his ancient foster-father Hǫrðr for an interpretation. Wisely, Hǫrðr refuses to board the ship and talk to Ívarr in person; instead he stands on a rock and they converse through the flap of Ívarr's tent. Hǫrðr says that Ívarr knows perfectly well what the dream means (54):

> ok meiri ván, at skammt líði heðan, áðr skipask munu ríki í Svíþjóð ok Danmǫrk, ok er nú kominn á þik helgráðr, er þú hyggsk ǫll ríki munu undir þik leggja, en þú veizt eigi, at hitt mun fram koma, at þú munt vera dauðr, en óvinir þínir munu fá ríkit.

> and there is greater hope that it will be only a short time from now before the rule of Sweden and Denmark will change, and now a fatal hunger is come upon you, because you thought all realms would submit to you, but you do not know that it will come to pass that you will be dead, and your enemies will obtain the realm.

Here an Eddic dialogue begins. Like Óðinn in pursuit of knowledge, Ívarr seeks information about his relatives from Hǫrðr: 'If so-and-so were one of the gods, which one would he be?' Hǫrðr supplies the equivalents one by one, but each answer ends with a negative remark about Ívarr himself (54–55), as in the first exchange:

> Konungr mælti: 'Hverr er Hálfdan snjalli með Ásum?' Hǫrðr svarar: 'Hann var Baldr með Ásum, er ǫll regin grétu, ok þér ólíkr.'

> The king spoke: 'Who is [my father] Hálfdan the Eloquent among the Æsir?' Hǫrðr answers, 'Among the Æsir he was Baldr, whom all the gods mourned, and unlike you.'

Twice a kind of refrain is interjected (54–55):

> Konungr mælti: 'Gakk hingat ok seg illspár þínar.' Hǫrðr mælti: 'Hér mun ek standa ok heðan segja.' ... 'Vel segir þú,' kvað konungr, 'gakk hingat ok seg tíðendi.' Hǫrðr svarar: 'Hér mun ek standa ok heðan segja.'

> The king spoke: 'Come here and say your evil prophecy.' Hǫrðr spoke: 'Here I will stand, and from here [I will] speak.' ...'You speak well,' uttered the king, 'Come here and say [your] tidings.' Hǫrðr answers: 'Here I will stand, and from here [I will] speak.'

Similar questions about his son-in-law Hrœrekr, about Hrœrekr's brother Helgi inn hvassi and about Ívarr's uncle Guðrøðr follow. Finally, Ívarr asks about himself (55):

> Konungr mælti: 'Hverr em ek með Ásum?' Hǫrðr svarar: 'Muntu vera ormr sá, sem verstr er til, er heitir Miðgarðsormr.'

> The king spoke: 'Who am I among the Æsir?' Hǫrðr answers: 'You would be that serpent who is the worst in existence, who is called Miðgarðsormr.'

Ívarr becomes so angry that he charges out of the tent and leaps at him, but Hǫrðr steps off his rock into the sea, and neither one of them surfaces afterwards. Whatever is going on here, it is not rationalisation.

Other significant additions and substitutions

Sǫgubrot thus minimises Óðinn's original role in the battle of Brávellir but supplies strong Odinic echoes in the previous generation. As all these events take place before the conversion of Denmark, the elaborate restructuring of the pagan presence might appear pointless, but I believe it can be explained in the light of other significant changes that the saga author makes.

These changes are curiously anachronistic. First, Haraldr's mother is described in such a way as to invoke echoes of the Icelandic settler Auðr in djúpúðga. Second, she is described in such a way as to invoke echoes of Ástríðr, the Norwegian mother of the missionary king Óláfr Tryggvason. Whoever Haraldr's mother was according to the original tradition, *Sǫgubrot* calls her Auðr/Unnr and gives her the nickname *in djúpúðga* 'the subtle' (52). Possibly it is significant that *Sǫgubrot* diverges in this regard from most of the earlier accounts. *Skjǫldunga saga* makes no mention of any of Ívarr's children, and in *Ynglinga saga* Snorri says nothing of Ívarr's having a daughter and instead states that he has a son named Óláfr (*Heimskringla*, I 73). *Sǫgubrot* thus diverges from *Ynglinga saga* in three ways: it attributes the creation of the Viking empire to Hálfdan snjalli rather than to Ívarr, and it gives Ívarr a daughter and is silent about a son. If *Ágrip af sǫgu Danakonunga* is earlier than *Sǫgubrot*, then it is the first prose version of the myth of the Viking empire to follow *Hyndluljóð* and give Ívarr a daughter named Auðr in djúpúðga. In any case, Auðr lives up to her nickname, for when Hrœrekr has killed Helgi, she takes her son and summons warriors. After Ívarr kills Hrœrekr, he has to retreat before her greater number of men, and she leaves the country, taking Haraldr first to Eygotaland and then to Garðaríki. Here we have the parallel with the story of Óláfr Tryggvason, for when Queen Gunnhildr's agents attempt to seize the young prince (*Óláfs saga Tryggvasonar*, chs 3–4), Óláfr's mother spirits him out of Norway. Like Haraldr and Auðr, Óláfr and his mother first go to Sweden. After two years, she plans to join her brother in Russia, but on the way, they are attacked by pirates and young Óláfr is captured and sold as a slave. Providentially, Óláfr ends up safely in Russia after all (*Óláfs saga Tryggvasonar*, chs 7–8).

If Haraldr is a parallel of Óláfr Tryggvason, then the implication is that he is a kind of pre-Christian, and this suggestion is emphasised by the way in which he meets his end. Quite unlike Saxo's version of the legend, in which Haraldr is the hapless victim of Óðinn's malice, Sǫgubrot depicts Haraldr as setting up the battle of Brávellir so that he can die in combat and thus earn a place in Valhalla. The effect is one of pagan martyrdom, in so far as a martyr could be defined as someone who seeks a particular kind of violent death so that he or she will be rewarded in the next world. This is the first time that Óðinn is mentioned explicitly in Sǫgubrot: Haraldr declares that only he and Óðinn are familiar with the boar's-snout formation (63). Even though Haraldr thinks Óðinn has deserted him, he still dedicates all the fallen to Óðinn. Presumably the logic behind this is that Valhalla is the only desirable afterlife, so even if Óðinn has deserted Haraldr in this world, Haraldr should still try to reach the pagan paradise. It is Haraldr himself who asks Hringr to fight him. The purpose of the battle is to get Haraldr a kingly death rather than an ignominious one, and Haraldr candidly tells Hringr that the Danes thought him too old and had planned to kill him in his bath (60). Hringr apparently agrees to stage a battle, the events at Brávellir unfold accordingly, and after Haraldr is killed, Hringr takes great care over the treatment of Haraldr's body and its burial, to ensure that he gets to Valhalla (361). It is difficult to know whether or not to make anything of Hringr's behaviour, but the battle is certainly not due to Óðinn's malice.

As if this vision of history were not complicated enough, the saga author makes a third change to the original legend. In addition to paralleling Óláfr Tryggvason, Haraldr hilditǫnn is also made to resemble Haraldr hárfagri, who as a youth vows that he will *eignazk allan Nóreg* 'come to possess all Norway' (*Heimskringla*, I 97). The full account of the conquest (*Haralds saga hárfagra*, chs 4–6) does not need to be repeated, but the following passage may have served as a model for the author of Sǫgubrot (*Heimskringla*, I 98):

> Þeir [Haraldr hárfagri ok Guthormr hertogi] fengu enga mótstǫðu, fyrr en þeir kómu til Orkadals. Þar var samnaðr fyrir þeim. Þar áttu þeir ina fyrstu orrostu við konung þann, er Grýtingr hét. Haraldr konungr fekk sigr, en Grýtingr var handtekinn ok drepit mikit lið af honum, en hann gekk til handa Haraldi konungi ok svarði honum trúnaðareiða. Eptir þat gekk allt fólk undir Harald konung í Orkdœlafylki ok gerðusk hans menn . . . Hann setti jarl í hverju fylki, þann er dœma skyldi lǫg ok landsrétt ok heimta sakeyri ok landskyldir, ok skyldi jarl hafa þriðjung skatta ok skylda til borðs sér ok kostnaðar.

> They [Haraldr hárfagri and Duke Guthormr] met no opposition until they came to Orkadalr. There before them was a levy. Their first battle was there, with a king who was named Grýtingr. King Haraldr won the victory, and Grýtingr was captured and a large force of his was killed, and he surrendered to King Haraldr and swore oaths of fealty to him. After that, all the people

in the Orkadal district submitted to King Harald and became his men... He set up a jarl in each district, whose duty was to render legal judgements and administer the laws of the land and to collect fines and renders, and a jarl was to have a third of the taxes and renders to support himself.

Like Haraldr hárfagri, Haraldr hilditǫnn is a young man when he embarks on a campaign of conquest (Sǫgubrot, 56–57):

> Haraldr var þá fimmtán vetra, er hann var til ríkis tekinn... Hann eignaðisk með orrostum ok hernaði ǫll þau ríki, er átt hafði Ívarr konungr, ok því meira, at engi konungr var sá í Danmǫrk eða Svíþjóð, at eigi gyldi honum skatt, ok allir gerðusk hans menn... Hann setti konunga ok jarla ok lét sér skatta gjalda.

> Haraldr was fifteen when he was accepted as ruler... With battles and raids he came to possess all those realms that King Ívarr had possessed, and more than that: there was no king in Denmark or Sweden who did not pay him a tax, and all became his men... He set up kings and jarls and had them pay taxes to him.

A further parallel between Haraldr hárfagri and Haraldr hilditǫnn emerges at the end of their reigns. In his old age, Haraldr hárfagri elevates Eiríkr blóðøx to the rank of king, but soon Haraldr's other sons have claimed parts of Norway for themselves (Haralds saga hárfagra, ch. 41). Haraldr hilditǫnn's realm is also divided when he is advanced in years: he makes Hringr king of Uppsala and gives him the government of all Sweden and west Gautland, but he retains the rule of Denmark and east Gautland for himself (58).

The late thirteenth-century political context

What are we to make of this multi-layered history, in which Iceland and two different Norwegian kings are projected onto a figure from legendary Denmark? We might look to the saga's contemporary political context in search of an interpretation, but it is not possible to date *Sǫgubrot* with any accuracy. All we know is that it is earlier than the manuscript from around 1300 in which it is preserved, and that its style suggests a date of after 1250 (Bjarni Guðnason 1982, xl). Possibly relevant is the fact that *Ragnars saga loðbrókar*, which is also dated to the second half of the thirteenth century (McTurk 1977, 568), shares with *Sǫgubrot* a negative depiction of the Swedes. In *Ragnars saga*, King Eysteinn of Sweden is described as *illgjarn* 'wicked, ill-natured' (*Ragnars saga loðbrókar*, 242), and the Swedish people worship the cow Síbilia, who is characterised by *svá mikill djöfuls kraftr* 'such great power of the devil' (*Ragnars saga loðbrókar*, 242). In *Sǫgubrot*, of course, the Swedish Ívarr acts like Óðinn and is literally said to be an evil monster. As King Hákon Magnússon of Norway (r. 1299–1319) betrothed his infant daughter to the duke of Sweden in 1302, the negative characterisation of the Swedes suggests that *Sǫgubrot* was written before this turn of events. Conversely, *Þáttr af Ragnars sonum*, which is believed to date from the early fourteenth century, rehabilitates the Swedes in its version of the legend of Ragnarr loðbrók (Rowe 2009, 356–57).

However, the contemporary political context does not suggest any reasons why the Swedes should be depicted in this way. Hákon sought good relations with Sweden well before 1302, and his father, Magnús lagabœtir (r. 1263–80), had worked constructively with his Swedish counterpart, Valdemar Birgisson (r. 1275–90), to define the border between Norway and Sweden for the first time. We are forced to conclude that just as the author of *Sǫgubrot* is not particularly interested in Danish-Swedish history for its own sake, neither is he particularly interested in using the legendary past as a mirror of the present.

The cultural context

One thing that is clear is the saga author's antiquarian bent. Mythological poetry is one of his interests; in addition to his use of *Brávallaþula* and *Hyndluljóð*, he may have been drawing on a poem that is now lost for the dialogue between Ívarr and Hǫrðr, as was suggested by Cleasby and Vigfusson, who in their citation of the use of the word *helgráðr* 'voracity betokening death' state that it is found in a paraphrase of a poem (Cleasby and Vigfusson 1957, 255a). Just as a metrical *þula* underlies the account of the battle of Brávellir, extensive alliteration in this passage suggests that it was drawn from a verse source.[8] If a lost poem was not the source for this dialogue, then the author would seem to be playing with Eddic conventions. Poems about attempts to win knowledge—especially knowledge regarding identities—from reluctant seers include *Hyndluljóð* and *Baldrs draumar*, and *Grímnismál* contains two instances of a phrase very similar to the central phrase of the dialogue in *Sǫgubrot* (e.g. *Hverr er Hálfdan snjalli með Ásum?* 'Who is Hálfdan the Eloquent among the Æsir?') In st. 49 of *Grímnismál* it appears as *Grímni mic héto at Geirraðar, en . . . Gǫndlir ok Hárbarðr með goðom* 'They called me Grímnir at Geirrøð's [hall], but . . . [they called me] Gǫndlir and Hárbarðr among the gods' (*Edda*, 67). In st. 54 it appears as *hétomc Þundr fyr þat . . . Gautr ok Iálcr*

---

[8] Alliteration appears in the following phrases: *Hér mun ek standa ok heðan segja* (54), *Hverr er Hálfdan snjalli með Ásum* (54), *Hverr var Hrœrekr með Ásum* (55), *Hann var Hœnir, er hræddastr var Ása* (55), *Hverr var Helgi inn hvassi með Ásum* (55), *Hann var Hermóðr, er bazt var hugaðr* (55), *Heimdallr var hann, er heimskastr var allra Ása* (55), *Hverr em ek með Ásum* (55), *Muntu vera ormr sá, sem verstr er til, er heitir Miðgarðsormr* (55) and *þrúðna þursinn* (55).

með goðom 'Before that they called me Þundr . . . [Before that they called me] Gautr and Iálcr among the gods' (*Edda*, 68). Even the disappearance of Ívarr and Hǫrðr into the sea—*sá þat síðast til konungs ok Harðar, at hvárrgi kom upp síðan* 'the last that [the watchmen on the king's ship] saw of the king and Hǫrðr [was] that neither of them came up later' (55)—is reminiscent of Eddic interlocutors who sink down into the earth after they have finished speaking, as in *Vǫluspá* and *Helreið Brynhildar*.

Brávallaþula and *Hyndluljóð* may perhaps be considered old lore to some degree, but the saga author includes younger sources as well, for in his description of the young Ragnarr loðbrók, there is a digression regarding Ragnarr's descent from Álfr gamli (70):

> Hann [Ragnarr] var allra þeira manna mestr ok fríðastr, er menn hefði sét, ok var hann líkr móður sinni ásýndar ok í hennar ætt at sjá, því at þat er kunnigt í ǫllum fornum frásǫgnum um þat fólk, er Álfar hétu, at þat var miklu fríðara en engi ǫnnur mannkind á Norðrlǫndum, því at allt foreldri Álfhildar, móður hans, ok allr ættbálkr var kominn frá Álfi gamla. Þat váru þá kallaðar Álfa ættir. Af honum tóku nǫfn þær tvær meginár, er elfr heitir hvártveggi síðan. Ǫnnur skildi ríki hans af Gautlandi, var sú fyrir því kǫlluð Gautelfr, en ǫnnur fell af því landi, er nú heitir Raumaríki, ok heitir sú Raumelfr.

> He [Ragnarr] was the tallest and handsomest of all the men that people had seen, and he was like his mother in appearance and clearly from her lineage, because it is known in all the old accounts about the people who are called Álfar that they are much handsomer than any other kind of men in the northern lands, because all of his mother Álfhildr's ancestors and that entire part of his family was descended from Álfr the Old. It was called the lineage of elves then. From him those two major rivers—each of which has been named Álfr [Elbe] ever since—took their names. One divided his realm from Gautland; this one was for that reason called Gautelfr, but the other flowed out of the country that is now called Raumaríki, and this one is called Raumelfr.

Bjarni Guðnason (1982, xli) supposes that this material is drawn from some redaction of *Ragnars saga loðbrókar*, but a version of it is also found at the beginning of *Þorsteins saga Víkingssonar* (1):

> Hann [Álfr inn gamli] réð fyrir því ríki, er liggr í milli á tveggja. Þær tóku nafn af honum, ok var kǫlluð elfr hvártveggi. Var sú kǫlluð Gautelfr, er fyrir sunnan var við land Gauta konungs ok skildi við Gautland. En sú var kǫlluð Raumelfr, er fyrir norðan var ok kennd var við Raum konung. Ríki þat var kallat Raumaríki. Þat váru kallaðir Álfheimar, er Álfr konungr réð fyrir, en þat folk er allt álfakyns, er af honum er komit. Váru þat fríðari menn en aðrar þjóðir næst risafólki.

> He [Álfr the Old] ruled over the realm that lies between them. These [rivers] took their names from him, and each of the two was called *elfr* [Elbe]. The one that was south of the land of King Gauti and formed the border with Gautland was called Gautelfr. And the one that was to the north and was known by King Raumr's name

was called Raumelfr. That realm was called Raumaríki. The one that King Álfr ruled over was called Álfheimar, and the people who are descended from him are all of elfkind. Those were the most handsome people after the giant folk.

Þorsteins saga Víkingssonar seems to have been composed approximately between 1280 and 1290 (Rowe 2004, 151–52), and the phrase *í ǫllum fornum frásǫgnum um þat fólk, er Álfar hétu* 'in all the old accounts about the people who are called Álfar', which is present in *Sǫgubrot* but absent in *Þorsteins saga Víkingssonar*, suggests that the former was borrowing from the latter, if they were not both drawing on a common exemplar. A similar phrase—*sem segir í ǫllum fornum sǫgum* 'as it says in all the old sagas' (65)—indicates that the author of *Sǫgubrot* was using material from a number of sources. It also implies that *Sǫgubrot* is not an 'old saga' itself.

Guðrún Nordal observes that in the thirteenth century, Icelandic poets and historians changed their focus from Danish myths and legends to Norwegian ones. This happened not only because the new political situation of submission to Norway lent 'weight and appeal' to Norwegian material (Nordal 2001, 326) but also because Denmark had ceased to be a market for Icelandic literary products. By around 1300, Icelandic textual culture functioned within a Norwegian milieu. *Sǫgubrot* exemplifies this transition, for although the subject of the narrative is East Norse legendary history, the Danes and Swedes who figure in it are given West Norse alter egos.

Conclusion

Bjarni Guðnason (1982, xli) regards *Sǫgubrot* as a rewriting and expansion of *Skjǫldunga saga* that was carried out in the second half of the thirteenth century as a result of the same cultural impulses that gave rise to the *fornaldarsögur*. 'Breyttur smekkur, nýjar sögur' (changed tastes, new sagas), he remarks. This conclusion results from an analysis of *Sǫgubrot*'s style that finds signifigant influence from romance. Bjarni is certainly correct in this regard, and to his list of chivalric inflections such as the battle descriptions and the *turniment* 'tournament' (51) (Bjarni Guðnason 1982, xxxix–xl) one could also add Hrœrekr's dream of a *hlébarðr* 'leopard' (50).[9] Nonetheless, although *Sǫgubrot* does reflect the cultural milieu of late thirteenth-century Iceland, changed tastes alone cannot account for the saga author's other reworkings of his source material. What would explain the omission of Óðinn from so much of the story, when Óðinn's role is left intact in

---

[9] Bjarni Guðnason (1982, xl) suggests that although *Þiðriks saga af Bern* may have served as a model in this regard, most probably general influence from romance is at work here.

Vǫlsunga saga, which cannot be more than a few decades older?[10] Indeed, what would explain the intrusion of Odinic motifs into the borrowings from romance? In the tournament referred to above, for example, a grim and incongruous note is struck by the contrast between the chivalric Helgi, who jousts *með burtstǫng* 'with a lance' (51), and his brother Hrœrekr, who equips himself unromantically with a helmet, byrnie, sword and spear. When the saga author has Hrœrekr run Helgi through with his spear, he is clearly doing something more than bringing the weaponry up to date.

It is important to remember that the text of *Sǫgubrot* is fragmentary, so a unified interpretation is not justifiable. It is also quite likely that what the saga author does is largely dictated by the pre-existing legends, from which he simply cannot stray very far. He can pursue the legend in this direction or that according to a genealogical framework that probably offers some scope for modification, and he can give a particular emphasis to specific episodes, but the overall action (Haraldr and Hringr fight, Haraldr is killed, Hringr fathers Ragnarr) is probably not mutable. Nonetheless, a partial interpretation may be ventured upon.

Haraldr hilditǫnn seems to be attracting two sets of parallels: one with Haraldr hárfagri, and the other with Óláfr Tryggvason. With the former, there is then an allusion to a specifically Norwegian tradition of empire-building. Even though Haraldr hilditǫnn's father was Danish and the dissolved empire he reconstructs was a Swedish creation, making Haraldr hilditǫnn into a prefiguration of Haraldr hárfagri endows Norwegian empire-building with an authoritative, ancient prehistory that is not surprising in a text compiled in the late thirteenth century, when Norwegian power encompassed Greenland, Iceland, Orkney, the Færoes and the Shetland Islands. The parallels with Óláfr Tryggvason turn Haraldr into a kind of pagan martyr, a person whose goal is to die in such a way as to enter his version of heaven. This might explain why Óðinn's role is diminished with respect to Haraldr, for if Haraldr is to be cast as a pre-Christian martyr, he should not also be depicted as a devoted worshipper of the foremost of the pagan gods. However, Óðinn's role in the original legend of the battle of Brávellir, to stir up emnity between family members, does not disappear from the narrative but is displaced to the previous generation, when Ívarr víðfaðmi maliciously induces Hrœrekr to kill his brother. The Odinisation of Ívarr, the previous pagan king, fits into the usual pattern in which an old, unredeemed generation is contrasted with a new generation that is either pre-Christian or ready for

---

[10] Finch (1993, 711a) dates *Vǫlsunga saga* to no later than around 1260–1270.

conversion.[11] Possibly this is a nested typology, in which the pagan age itself is divided into an evil old half and a less evil new half, but more likely it represents a multi-stage development towards Christianity, in that the oldest generation is suggested to be the pagan gods reborn, the next generation hopes only to attain the best afterlife, and the account of the third generation opens with ominous references to sacrifices and epidemics in Norway (71):

> Þá er Sigurðr hringr var gamall, var þat á einu hausti, er hann hafði riðit um ríki sitt, Gautland vestra, at dœma mǫnnum landslǫg, ok þá kómu í móti honum Gandálfssynir, mágar hans, ok báðu, at hann mundi veita þeim lið at ríða á hendr þeim konungi, er Eysteinn het, er því ríki réð, er þá hétu Vestmarar, en nú heitir Vestfold. Þá váru hǫfð blót í Skíringssal, er til var sótt um alla Víkina.
>
> When Sigurðr hringr was old, it happened one autumn, when he was riding around his realm, West Gautland, to pass sentences on people according to the laws of the land, his kinsmen, the sons of Gandálfr, came up to him and asked him to give them a party of men with which to ride against a king who was named Eysteinn, who ruled the realm that was then called Vestmarr but is now called Vestfold. Sacrifices had been held in Skíringssalr, as there was sickness all across Víkin.

The fragment breaks off at this point, but possibly the saga would have gone on to tell how active pagan practices were eradicated.

The demonising of the Swedish Ívarr víðfaðmi suggests a time of composition roughly that of *Ragnars saga loðbrókar*, before 1300, when the king of Norway betrothed his daughter to the duke of Sweden. However, the author of *Sǫgubrot* seems to be less interested in using legendary Scandinavia as a mirror of the present than he is in using legendary Scandinavia as a vehicle for exploring Icelandic-Norwegian relations. The analysis presented here begins with the battle of Brávellir, but the changes that the saga author makes to his account of that battle are the logical development of the changes that he made earlier in the narrative. First Ívarr víðfaðmi is Odinised, and then Auðr and Haraldr hilditǫnn are depicted as parallels of Ástríðr and Óláfr Tryggvason. The saga author next omits Óðinn from the explanation for Haraldr's invulnerability to iron, and immediately afterward Haraldr is made to resemble Haraldr hárfagri. Only then does the saga author write Óðinn out of the battle of Brávellir. As Bjarni Guðnason (1958, 116) points out, of the two versions of the battle, the one in which the battle comes about because Óðinn has sown strife between kinsmen is doubtless the original; Haraldr's desire to die in battle rather than of old age must be a very young motif. Here I would add that the reason why

---

[11] Examples of this pattern are provided by Schach (1977), Harris (1986) and Rowe (2005, 68–73).

the original version had to be changed was because it undermined the parallelism between Haraldr hilditǫnn and Óláfr Tryggvason.

Just as Saxo seems to have felt that Icelanders belonged at the battle of Brávellir, the saga author too appears to think that Iceland ought not to be left out of the heroic past. But where Saxo seems to be including Icelandic names because he envisions the combatants as coming from all over Scandinavia, the saga author uses a single Icelandic name to make grandiose implications about how much Norway owes to her new tributary country. When Auðr is positioned as the mother of a figure who resembles Haraldr hárfagri, the parallelism suggests that an Icelander helped create the very existence of Norway as a state. When Auðr herself is made to resemble the mother of Óláfr Tryggvason—and not merely a parallel to Ástríðr, but a superior version of her, one who actually succeeds in getting her son to Russia—the parallelism suggests that an Icelander was responsible for saving the agent of Norway's own salvation.[12] And when an Icelander crafts a saga about legendary Scandinavia from a *þula*, pagan mythology, and one or more Eddic poems, he seems to be suggesting that Iceland is the guardian of the cultural heritage of the north. And that, at least, is not so very far from the truth.

Bibliography

Bjarni Aðalbjarnarson 1941–51. 'Formali'. In Snorri Sturluson. *Heimskringla*. Ed. Bjarni Aðalbjarnarson. Íslenzk fornrit XXVI–XXVIII, XXVI v–cxl.

Bjarni Guðnason 1958. 'Um Brávalla þulu'. *Skírnir* 132, 82–128.

Bjarni Guðnason 1982. 'Formáli'. In *Danakonunga sǫgur*. Íslenzk fornrit XXXV, v–cxciv.

Cleasby, Richard and Gudbrand Vigfusson 1957. *An Icelandic-English Dictionary*. 2nd ed. With a supplement by William A. Craigie.

Degnbol, Helle et al., eds, 1989. *A Dictionary of Old Norse Prose / Ordbog over det norrøne prosasprog*. *Indices / Registre*.

Ellis Davidson, Hilda, ed., and Peter Fisher, trans., 1979–80. *Saxo Grammaticus. The History of the Danes, Books I–IX*.

Finch, R. G. 1993. 'Vǫlsunga saga'. In *Medieval Scandinavia: An Encyclopedia*. Ed. Phillip Pulsiano et al., 711.

Hald, Kristian 1975. 'Navnestoffet hos Saxo'. *Saxostudier: Saxo-kollokvierne ved Københavns universitet*. Ed. Ivan Boserup, 79–94.

Harris, Joseph 1986. 'Saga as historical novel'. In *Structure and Meaning in Old Norse Literature: New Approaches to Textual Analysis and Literary Criticism*. Ed. John Lindow, Lars Lönnroth and Gerd Wolfgang Weber, 187–219.

---

[12] A later work, *Orms þáttr Stórólfssonar*, explores a similar theme when the Icelander Ormr Stórólfsson is declared to have been so strong that if he had been with Óláfr Tryggvason in his last battle, the king's ship would never have been taken by the enemy (Rowe 2005, 67–68, 83–84).

Heimskringla = Snorri Sturluson, *Heimskringla* 1941–51. Ed. Bjarni Aðalbjarnarson. Íslenzk fornrit XXVI–XXVIII.

Hollander, Lee M., trans., 1962. *The Poetic Edda*. 2nd. rev. ed.

Jón Helgason, ed., 1924. *Heiðreks saga: Hervarar saga ok Heiðreks konungs*. Samfund til udgivelse af gammel nordisk litteratur XLVIII.1.

McTurk, Rory 1977. 'The relationship of *Ragnars saga loðbrókar* to *Þiðriks saga af Bern*'. In *Sjötíu ritgerðir helgaðar Jakobi Benediktssyni 20. júli 1977*. Ed. Einar G. Pétursson and Jónas Kristjánsson, 568–85.

Nordal, Guðrún 2001. *Tools of Literacy: The Role of Skaldic Verse in Icelandic Textual Culture of the Twelfth and Thirteenth Centuries*.

Nordal, Sigurður, ed., 1944. *Flateyjarbók* I.

Olrik, A. 1894. 'Bråvalla kvadets Kæmperække'. *Arkiv för nordisk filologi* 10, 223–87.

Olrik, Axel 1919. *The Heroic Legends of Denmark*.

Edda = *Edda: Die Lieder des Codex Regius nebst verwandten Denkmälern* 1962. Ed. G. Neckel, rev. H. Kuhn. 4th edition.

Pritsak, Omeljan 1993. 'Hervarar saga og Heiðreks konungs'. In *Medieval Scandinavia: An Encyclopedia*. Ed. Phillip Pulsiano et al., 283a–b.

Ragnars saga loðbrókar. In *Fornaldarsögur norðurlanda* 1954, I–IV. Ed. Guðni Jónsson. Vol. 1.

Rowe, Elizabeth Ashman 2004. 'Absent Mothers and the Sons of Fornjótr: Late-Thirteenth-Century Monarchist Ideology in *Þorsteins saga Víkingssonar*'. *Mediaeval Scandinavia* 14, 133–60.

Rowe, Elizabeth Ashman 2005. *The Development of Flateyjarbók: Iceland and the Norwegian Dynastic Crisis of 1389*.

Rowe, Elizabeth Ashman 2009. '*Ragnars saga loðbrókar*, *Ragnarssona þáttr*, and the Political World of Haukr Erlendsson'. In *Fornaldarsagaerne: Myter og virkelighed*, ed. Agneta Ney, Ármann Jakobsson and Annette Lassen, 347–60.

Schach, Paul 1977. 'Some Observations on the Generation-Gap Theme in the Icelandic Sagas'. In *The Epic in Medieval Society: Aesthetic and Moral Values*. Ed. Harald Scholler, 361–81.

Seip, Didrik Arup 1927. 'Den norske grunnlag for Bråvallakvadet hos Saxo'. *Norsk tidsskrift for sprogvidenskap* 3, 1–20.

Skjǫldunga saga. In *Danakonunga sǫgur* 1982. Ed. Bjarni Guðnason. Íslenzk fornrit XXXV.

Skovgaard-Petersen, Inge 1987. *Da Tidernes Herre var nær: Studier i Saxos historiesyn*.

Skovgaard-Petersen, Inge 1993. 'Brávallaþula'. In *Medieval Scandinavia: An Encyclopedia*, ed. Phillip Pulsiano et al., 56–57.

Stefán Karlsson 1975. 'Diskussion'. In *Saxostudier: Saxo-kollokvierne ved Københavns universitet* Ed. Ivan Boserup, 91–93.

Sǫgubrot. In *Danakonunga sǫgur* 1982. Ed. Bjarni Guðnason. Íslenzk fornrit XXXV.

Turville-Petre, E. O. G. 1964. *Myth and Religion of the North: The Religion of Ancient Scandinavia*.

Wolf, Kirsten 1993. 'Skjǫldunga saga'. In *Medieval Scandinavia: An Encyclopedia*. Ed. Phillip Pulsiano et al., 597–98.

Þorsteins saga Víkingssonar. In *Fornaldarsögur norðurlanda* 1954 I–IV. Ed. Guðni Jónsson. Vol. 3.

HRÓLFS SAGA KRAKA AND THE LEGEND OF LEJRE

TOM SHIPPEY

In his entry on *Hrólfs saga kraka* in *Medieval Scandinavia: an Encyclopedia*, Jonathan Evans remarks that 'next to *Vǫlsunga saga* [it is] probably the best-known of the *fornaldarsögur*' (Evans 1993, 304), a view confirmed by the existence of three modern English translations (Jones 1961, Byock 1998 and Tunstall 2003). Its popularity in earlier times is shown by the number of manuscripts extant, the list of 38 compiled by Slay (1960) having been further extended to 59 by Driscoll and Hufnagel (2009). All the manuscripts are thought to go back to one common original, which may be the copy listed as extant at Möðruvellir in 1461, though legends about the hero were in wide circulation throughout Scandinavia much earlier.

The saga's popularity in modern times may, however, give a rather false impression, for much of it derives from the fact that the saga is an analogue of the Old English poem *Beowulf*. There is no doubt that its hero Hrólfr is to be identified with the enigmatic and unspeaking figure of Hrothulf, mentioned twice in the much older Old English epic, though there he plays no active part at all. Both men are said to be members of the Skjǫldungr or Scylding dynasty, and poem and saga furthermore share at least seven other characters. Much of the commentary on the saga has accordingly dealt with its relationship to *Beowulf*, as one can see from the bibliographies given by Evans and Driscoll / Hufnagel, while much of the remainder deals with single motifs, such as its ursine elements (Tolley 2007) or its 'perilous women' (Ármann Jakobsson 2003). Two issues have been dealt with relatively rarely. First, the saga has not often been considered as a whole and for itself. Second, till very recently interest had faded in the saga's connection with its many Scandinavian analogues, both earlier and later.

This latter situation has, however, changed both recently and dramatically. Scandinavian stories of Hrólfr agree in placing him and his dynasty at a place variously labelled as Lethra, Hledro, Hleiðra or (the saga's form) Hleiðargarðr; and it has long been agreed that this must be the small village near Roskilde now known as Lejre, or Gammel Lejre. It has nevertheless also been agreed for most of the last century that there is no historical basis for what, following

Niles (2007), may be called the 'legend of Lejre'. Gwyn Jones, for instance, after brilliantly summing up the Skjǫldungr legends, remarks that

> of Hrolf's sixth-century court no trace has been found. It is sad to think of those high lords without a roof to their heads, but in respect of Lejre that is the case, and likely to remain so. (Jones 1968, 46–47)

H. R. Ellis Davidson repeated the point with equal assurance some years later in her commentary on a new translation of Saxo Grammaticus, observing that 'there is no reason to suppose' Lejre was of any importance at the time Hrólfr was supposed to live (Ellis Davidson and Fisher 1979, II 46). The 'legend of Lejre' had in fact been written off as mere fable.

But then the archaeologists took a hand. In the late 1980s excavations began on the Lejre site under the direction of the archaeologist Tom Christensen, with further work continuing to the present day, and these excavations revealed not one but three massive halls on two different sites, dating from the mid-sixth century up to the eleventh. One of these, Christensen notes, found in the first site excavated during the 1980s, is 'the largest we yet know of from the Late Germanic Iron Age and the Viking period' (Christensen 1991, 73); while the earliest of the halls, almost as long but not as wide, and found on the second site excavated during the 2000s, nevertheless 'must be classed among the very largest buildings known from the sixth century in Denmark' (Christensen 2005, 122). Furthermore, and reported only after this paper was first presented and as it was about to go to press, news has come in of a third site excavated at Lejre which has produced yet another hall complex, with as many as three halls built successively, the largest of them even larger than anything so far discovered, almost 200 feet long. Not enough of this last discovery is known yet for any comment to be made on it. However, one has to say that in the current state of knowledge, the dates of legend and archaeology do not entirely match, for if we were to go by the (uncertain) evidence of *Beowulf*, Hrólfr's period of power ought to have been the earlier sixth century, i.e. just before Christensen's earliest hall was built. But there is no doubt, at least, that—just as the various forms of the 'legend of Lejre' asserted—Lejre was a major power-centre for Scandinavia before and lasting into the Viking era. The question has accordingly resurfaced, 'Ha[ve] modern scholars been too hasty in writing off the kings of Lejre?' (Christensen 1991, 21). And can anything be deduced from the legend as a whole, *Hrólfs saga* included?

This essay accordingly seeks to do two things. First, albeit briefly, to consider the saga as a whole and for itself. Second, to review the saga's connections with the other Scandinavian versions of the 'legend of Lejre', but not (except for one brief lapse) with *Beowulf*.

The Structure of the Saga: Gaps and Failings

There is no doubt that the saga author is capable of arresting and entertaining narrative, but the saga as a whole is not well-structured. It consists of some six or more not very well integrated units, some but not all of them marked off as separate sections in Guðni Jónsson's 1954 edition. I number, identify and summarise these here for future convenience, with chapter numbers from this edition.

1) Chapters 1–5, 'Fróða þáttr': This says that there were two brothers, Hálfdan and Fróði. Fróði kills his brother, and tries to kill his two sons, Hróarr and Helgi, but they escape, and in the end avenge their father.

2) 6–17, 'Helga þáttr': This tells the story of the incestuous birth of Hrólfr. Helgi rapes a Saxon queen called Óløf, who bears a daughter whom she refuses to acknowledge, and to whom she gives the dog's name of Yrsa. Yrsa grows up to be an outstanding beauty, and Helgi carries her off and sires Hrólfr on her, without knowing who she is. Yrsa's mother bides her time, but eventually discloses the secret of the couple's incest, after which Yrsa is married off to King Aðils of Sweden—who, in the end, kills Helgi, his predecessor.

Inserted in this story, however, are two further sequences:

2a) 10–12, the tale of Hróarr's ring: Helgi has a very valuable ring, which he gives to his brother Hróarr. The latter allows a cousin, Hrókr, to handle it, but Hrókr throws it in the sea. Hróarr mutilates Hrókr, but Hrókr kills Hróarr. Helgi takes further revenge on Hrókr, and Hróarr's posthumous child Agnarr retrieves the ring.

2b) 15, the elf-woman and the birth of Skuld: In this chapter, Helgi sires a child on an elf-woman, but fails to collect the child as agreed. The elf-woman nevertheless sends him his daughter, Skuld, and says a curse will be laid on his kinsfolk for his breach of their agreement.

3) 18–23, 'Svipdags þáttr': Svipdagr forces his way into the retinue of King Aðils and has conflicts with the king's berserks, in which he is assisted by his two brothers Beigaðr and Hvítserkr. They eventually decide, however, to serve King Hrólfr, because of the fame he has

acquired at Hleiðargarðr. The last chapter of this section, 23, tells how Hrólfr tricks Hjǫrvarðr, husband of his half-sister Skuld, into becoming his under-king.

4) 24–36, 'Bǫðvars þáttr' and 37, 'Hjalta þáttr': This is in effect a fairy-tale. Bǫðvarr is the son of a were-bear, the least monstrous of three brothers. He goes to take service with King Hrólfr, defeats the king's ill-mannered champions and rescues a man they are tormenting. Bǫðvarr then kills a dragon, and makes the man he has rescued drink its blood, after which the former weakling becomes bold and strong and is given the name Hjalti, as also the nickname *inn hugprúði* 'the magnanimous' for his forbearance in not taking revenge on his former tormentors.

5) 38–47, Hrólfr's raid on Uppsala and his return: Egged on by Bǫðvarr, Hrólfr rides to King Aðils's court at Uppsala to recover his *fǫðurarfr* 'patrimony'. He and his men evade various plots and ambushes, and ride off with much of Aðils's treasure, hotly pursued across the Fýrisvellir plain by Aðils. To escape, Hrólfr scatters the gold, so that the Swedes stop to pick it up, and Aðils himself bends from his horse to retrieve an especially valuable ring. At this Hrólfr exclaims, '*Svínbeygða ek nú þann, sem Svíanna er ríkastr*' "Now I 'swine-bowed' him who is mightiest of the Swedes", and slices off Aðils's buttocks. During the expedition, however, Hrólfr antagonises his former supporter Óðinn.

6) 47–42, the Last Stand and Fall of King Hrólfr and his men: Hrólfr is attacked at Hleiðargarðr by his half-sister Skuld and her husband Hjǫrvarðr. Before the battle, Hjalti 'the Magnanimous', seeing the enemy ships approach, asks his mistress whether she would prefer two men of twenty-two or one of eighty. She says the former, and he bites off her nose; he then goes to join the doomed battle. After this has lasted a while, Hjalti notices Bǫðvarr is not there, goes to find him, and urges him into the battle—but as he does so a great bear fighting in Hrólfr's ranks (obviously Bǫðvarr's were-shape) vanishes and is not seen again. The battle ends with Hjalti, Bǫðvarr and most of the other champions falling round their king, while Hjǫrvarðr dies as well, further vengeance being taken by Yrsa and Bǫðvarr's brothers on Skuld.

Some parts of this are certainly well told, perhaps especially section (4) above, 'Bǫðvars þáttr'. One can also see that the author has done his best to thread items together, for instance inserting the story of Skuld, and the story of the tricking of Hjǫrvarðr, in chs 15 and 23 respectively, thus providing a double motivation ahead of time for the Last Battle. However, there are also clear lacunae, 'blind motifs' (i.e. sections which seem to promise a continuation but in the end lead nowhere), as well as cases of apparently pointless 'doubling'.

To take the last item first, sections (3) and (4) above, Svipdagr and his two brothers, Bǫðvarr and his two brothers, look very like each other. In ch. 18 King Aðils's berserks challenge Svipdagr, asking *hvart hann sé kappi nokkurr* 'whether he is some kind of champion', and he answers, *slíkr sem nokkurr þeira einn* 'as much as any one of them'. In ch. 22, it is King Hrólfr's berserks who challenge him, going round the hall and asking each man *hvárt sá teldist jafnsnjallr honum* 'whether he rated himself as bold a man as he' and getting evasive but conciliatory answers—until they reach Svipdagr, who immediately jumps up and draws his sword. In ch. 37 the same scene is played out with Bǫðvarr. King Hrólfr's berserks go round the hall asking the same question and getting the same kind of answer, till they reach Bǫðvarr, who is asked the usual question and responds, '*ekki jafnsnjallr, heldr snjallari*' "not as bold, but bolder". In chs 22 and 37 brawls break out, though Hrólfr, unlike Aðils, forbids killing. (One has to say that the nameless berserks of both kings become rather tedious, *þóttust þó á honum ávallt meiri ok sátu ávallt á svikráðum við hann* 'forever thinking themselves stronger than [Bǫðvarr] and always laying plots against him' (ch. 49), but never actually amounting to much.) Svipdagr and his brothers also seem to fade out of the story. They are given places to King Hrólfr's left, Bǫðvarr and Hjalti being on his right (ch. 37); they are present on the Uppsala ride, and Svipdagr even calls in an earlier promise by Aðils to buy his companions temporary immunity (ch. 40); but they are only mentioned in the Last Stand sequence, along with seven other men, named but not individualised. Very little would be lost from the saga if the whole of section (3) were deleted, along with all further mentions of Svipdagr and his brothers.[1]

---

[1] Their connection with the 'legend of Lejre' as a whole is thin. Saxo mentions a Suipdagerus king of Norway in his Book 1, and a Svipdagr figures in the poem *Fjǫlsvinnsmál* (Ellis Davidson and Fisher 1979, II 28–29), but neither seems relevant. Beigaðr is mentioned once, in connection with Hrólfr, in *Tóka þáttr Tókasonar*.

As for 'blind motifs', one might wonder about the whole story of Hrókr and the precious ring. As things stand, the ring is thrown into the sea, but then recovered. No more is heard of Agnarr, except that Bǫðvarr, close to death, boasts of the services he has done for King Hrólfr, which include the fact that '*ek drap Agnar, berserk ok eigi síðr konung*' "I killed Agnarr, berserk and no less a king". Could they be the same man? Is Bǫðvarr boasting of killing Hrólfr's cousin for him? What happened to the ring? Even weaker, however, is the case of Vǫggr. He is introduced in ch. 42 as a servant of King Aðils, so it is odd that he cheekily gives Hrólfr the nickname *kraki* 'pole-ladder' (presumably because he is tall and thin). Hrólfr rewards him, the king says (not very relevantly), '*Litlu verðr Vöggr feginn*' "It doesn't take much to make Vǫggr happy" and Vǫggr swears (again, not very relevantly) to avenge the king if he outlives him, though not much notice is taken of this, for Vǫggr seems physically unimpressive. The *Litlu verðr . . .* saying is found also in Snorri's *Skáldskaparmál*, but Snorri does not complete the story. The whole sequence is told much better by Saxo Grammaticus, writing probably more than two centuries before the saga was written, where the whole point of the story is that Vǫggr is present at the Last Stand and the only one of Hrólfr's men to survive. Offered his life if he will swear fealty to Hjǫrvarðr the victor, he agrees, takes the latter's sword to swear on, but then runs the new king through with it, thus fulfilling his oath and ensuring that the usurper becomes king only for a few minutes, a satisfying and ironic conclusion. In the saga, though, there is none of this. Vǫggr is not even present at the Last Stand, Hjǫrvarðr is killed in the battle by Bǫðvarr, and all the saga author can say, remembering the promise to take vengeance, is that Yrsa sends men to take revenge on Skuld, *ok segja menn, at Vöggr hefði þar verit flokksforingi fyrir* 'men say that Vǫggr was the leader of the troop', by comparison with Saxo merely bathetic.

One could continue to make criticisms. The motivation of Yrsa is peculiar: she stays married to Aðils, but is continually hostile to him. The point of Hrólfr's visit to Uppsala is less than clear—to regain his *fǫðurarfr*, says Bǫðvarr, but one would have thought vengeance for Hrólfr's father Helgi would be a more pressing motive, for according to the saga he was killed by Aðils, though other versions of the Skjǫldungr epic have different explanations. One gets the impression that the saga author knows quite a lot of related tales, and is reluctant to leave anything out (hence Svipdagr and his brothers, Hrókr and the ring, the two Agnarrs). But at the same time he does not know the full story in some cases, and so has to make up his own conclusions, as with Vǫggr's unconvincing revenge, and the offstage and quickly forgotten death of Helgi.[2]

The biggest lacuna of the saga, however, is simply Hrólfr. He is presented as the great hero of the North, but as far as we can see, he does almost nothing. The chase across the Fýrisvellir plain was clearly famous (see below), but kings of the Danes do not normally gain glory by running away from the Swedes. The rest of the saga is not about him (except for the tale of his incestuous birth) but about his champions. The Old English poem *Widsiþ* does indeed credit him with a major feat: with his uncle Hroþgar he killed Ingeld and destroyed the Heaþo-Bard army 'at Heorot', Hroþgar's great hall. But if the event ever took place, the Heaþo-Bards were destroyed so completely that no one is now sure who they were, though some have suggested that their name survives in the southern Baltic area of Bardengau, and the name Hothbrodus—a tribal name converted to a personal one?—recurs uneasily in legendary tradition. However, *Hrólfs saga* itself knows nothing of this. The king is almost a *roi fainéant*—so much so that two critics have suggested independently that the saga may be in effect a satire on heroic pretensions (Valgerður Brynjólfsdóttir 2003 and Kalinke 2003). Certainly, in the saga's presentation of the king, one has to take the wish for the deed. The saga author was, of course, not the only medieval Icelander who had trouble arranging, and even understanding, his much older materials, but to these I now turn.

The Legend of Lejre

What were the earlier *frásagnir* 'narratives' about Hrólfr, mentioned by Snorri and from which the author of *Hrólfs saga* must have drawn? Obviously we cannot tell for sure, but it might be noted before proceeding further how similar are the situations of King Hrólfr and 'King Arthur'. Both men were active (if they existed at all) in the early sixth century. There is no contemporary documentation for either. In both cases the legends became established in the twelfth century, by Latin chroniclers, respectively Saxo (*c*.1200) and Geoffrey of Monmouth (*c*.1135). In both cases, though, there are hints of earlier knowledge in works now hard to

---

[2] No one gives a satisfying account of the death of Helgi, prominent in the legend though he is. Saxo suggests that he committed suicide from shame at his incest, *Skjǫldunga saga* and *Ynglinga saga* that he died in an unidentified battle, the *Lejre Chronicle* mentions his burial but not the manner of his death.

date, such as the *Gododdin* poem, surviving in Middle Welsh but thought to have been composed in a different place and dialect (see Koch 1997), or the fragments of the Old Norse poem *Bjarkamál* or 'Lay of [Bǫðvarr] Bjarki'. Both men attracted stories ascribed to their knights or champions, and both formed connections in legend with particular places, Hleiðra/ Lejre or the still unidentified Camelot. One could well add that in both cases there is still very deep reluctance by professional historians to take the legends seriously, but that—even allowing for the ninth-century evidence of the *Historia Brittonum* ascribed to 'Nennius', to which one could nevertheless oppose the uncertain witness of *Beowulf*—on the whole, the evidence for King Hrólfr is stronger than that for his more famous contemporary.

Once again leaving out *Beowulf* and *Widsiþ*, there are almost a dozen medieval Scandinavian accounts of Hrólfr other than the saga, which I enumerate here, in very brief outline, as far as possible in chronological order, and largely following the list compiled by Marijane Osborn and others (Niles 2007). More extensive selections from them may be found translated in Garmonsway et al. 1968, with original texts and a somewhat different set of selections in Fulk et al. 2008, 294–306.

1) *Grottasǫngr* (Old Norse poem, date unknown, possibly as old as 1000). Mentions *Hleiðrar stóli* in st. 20; st. 22 reads in part *mun Yrso sonr / við Hálfdana hefna Fróða; / sá mun hennar heitinn verða / burr oc bróðir* (see below for comment and translation).

2) *Bjarkamál* (Old Norse poem, said in the thirteenth century to have been old even in 1030, and apparently set at the moment of Hrólfr's Last Stand). Only some lines survive in Old Norse, plus a long Latin paraphrase in Saxo, (6) below. Similar to Hjalti's 'wake-up' call in ch. 49 of the saga.

3) *Langfeðgatal* (twelfth century). A royal genealogical list, part of which goes:

> Froðe frækni ... Ingialdr Starkaðar fostri h[ans] s[onr], Halfdan broðir hans, Helgo ok Hroar h. ss., Rolfr Kraki Helga s., Hrærekr Hnauggvanbaugi Iniallz s., Froðe h. s., Halfdan h. s., Hrærekr Slaungvanbaugi h. s.

> Fróði the Bold, father of Ingjaldr foster-son of Starkaðr, Hálfdan his brother; his sons Helgi and Hróarr, Hrólfr Kraki son of Helgi, Hrærekr Hnǫggvanbaugi Ingjaldr's son, his son Fróði, his son Hálfdan, his son Hrærekr Slǫngvanbaugi.

4) *The Lejre Chronicle* (Latin, late twelfth century): Ro was the son of Dan. His sons were Helgi and Haldanus. [Note: the version of this in *Gesta Danorum* inverts the genealogy so that Haldan is once again the

father of Helghe and Ro.] Tells the incestuous birth story, and Rolf's death at the hands of Hiarwart and Sculd.

5) Sven Aggesen, *Short History of the Kings of Denmark* (Latin, c. 1188): Skjold's heirs are Frothi and Haldanus, Haldanus kills Frothi, is succeeded in turn by Helghi, Rolf Kraki, 'killed at Lethra', and Rokil Slaghenback.

6) Saxo Grammaticus, *Gesta Danorum* (Latin, c.1200): Extensive account in Book 2 of Rolvo's incestuous birth, his raid on Uppsala, his death at the hands of Sculda and Hiarwarthus, and the revenge taken by his last surviving retainer Wiggo. Book 7 adds the story of Haldanus.

7) Snorri Sturluson, *Ynglinga saga* (Icelandic, early thirteenth century), tells of the incestuous birth, briefly mentions the battle on the ice of Lake Väner, the expedition to Uppsala, the sowing of gold on Fýrisvellir, and the death of Hrólfr at Hleiðra.

8) Snorri Sturluson, *Skáldskaparmál* (Icelandic, early thirteenth century): Kraki gives the boy Vǫggr a ring, in return for which he promises to avenge him. Snorri also gives the story of the Uppsala raid, the Fýrisvellir chase and the ring Svíagríss, including use of the verb *svínbeyga*.

9) *Annales Ryenses* (Latin, c.1290): Rolf killed at Leire by Hiartwarus, along with Biarki and Hjalti.

10) *Bjarkarímur* (Faeroese, c.1400): Hálfdan's sons are Hróarr and Helgi. The Hrœrekr 'Ring-slinger' story is told much as in the saga, but the ring is Svíagríss, and Agnarr is the son of Ingjaldr, not Hróarr, and is later killed by Bjarki. Also tells the story of Vǫggr's vow of vengeance.

11) *Skjǫldunga saga* (date unknown, survives only in Latin epitome by Arngrímr Jónsson, c.1570): Scioldo's grandson is Frodo; Rolfo Krake is born of incest (not detailed); his uncle Roas is killed by his own first cousins, Rærecus and Frodo, sons of Ingialldus; Rolfo is named Krake by Woggerus, who vows to avenge him; his champions are Witserchus and Bodvarus; the latter kills Agnarus, another son of Ingialldus. Rolfo helps Adillus to fight Alo on Lake Waener, but does not get paid, and raids Adillus to get his dues; the 'stoop like a swine' story is told; he is killed by Hiorvardus and Scullda, avenged by Woggerus, succeeded by Rærecus, see above.

In addition to the above, it should be noted that there are a number of references to Hrólfr in the *Íslendingasögur* and the *fornaldarsögur*, several of them mentioning Hrólfr's sword Skǫfnungr, said to have been looted from his barrow and taken to Iceland by Miðfjarðar-Skeggi.

The most obvious fact about the Scandinavian accounts, however, is that they are bewilderingly contradictory. There seems to be no certainty about who people are. Thus,

Hrólfs saga says at the start that Fróði kills Hálfdan. But Sven Aggesen and Saxo say that Haldanus kills Frothi; though Saxo (who seems to have dealt with conflicting accounts by telling both as if of different people) says that *another* Frothi tried to kill Haldanus.

The Eddic poem *Grottasǫngr* refers to the same conflict, but is hard to make out. In it two giantesses, enslaved by Fróði, rebel and threaten him with vengeance. Two lines of stanza 22 are given above (p. 24), and as they stand they mean 'the son of Yrsa will avenge Fróði on the Half-Danes; he will be known as her son and brother'. The reference to incest makes it certain that the 'son of Yrsa' is Hrólfr, but the rest does not fit well either with other accounts of the feud or with the poem's own context, in which the giantesses are threatening Fróði. It has been suggested that the second line should read *vígs Hálfdanar hefna Fróða* (Bugge 1867): Hrólfr will 'avenge the killing of Hálfdan on Fróði', better sense and better grammar. But if this was once the case the scribes of the poem did not understand it.

Furthermore:

The saga is clear that Hróarr is the son of Hálfdan, but the *Lejre Chronicle* says that Haldanus is the son of Ro. Very interestingly, however, the man who translated the chronicle into Old Danish, working with an authoritative Latin text in front of him, was aware enough of a different version to challenge it, writing that Haldan had two sons, *en het Ro—oc summe sighæ at han het Haldan—oc anner het Helghe* 'one was called Ro—but some say he was called Haldan—and the other was called Helgi' (Gordon 1962, 165).

There is a well-agreed ancestry for Hrólfr, but:

There is near-total disagreement about Fróði. The saga says he is the brother of Hálfdan, Saxo calls him the father of Haldanus, in the *Langfeðgatal* he appears both four names above and two names below Rolfr (along with two Halfdans and two Hrærekrs), in the *Lejre Chronicle* he is Rolf's grandson, and in the *Skjǫldunga saga* epitome he is Rolfo's cousin. Clearly there is a feeling that he should be in the story. But who is he?

Other figures bob around disquietingly, such as Hrærekr Slaungvanbaugi or 'Ring-Slinger', who must be the same as the saga's Hrókr, and who may well be the same as his namesake Hrærekr Hnauggvanbaugi, 'Ring-Miser'; Ingialdr (in the Old English tradition son of Froda and defeated by Hroþulf); Hothbrodus (who kills Ro in Saxo; it is suggested above that this is a tribal name converted to a personal one); and Agnarr or Agnerus, who never quite comes into focus, even in *Hrólfs saga*, see above.[3]

Nevertheless, one has to concede also that there are some areas of solid agreement centring on the life of Hrólfr himself:

The story of his incestuous birth is repeated with little variation in items (1), (4), (6), (7) and (11) above.

The Fýrisvellir chase also appears, this time with even some verbal consistency, in (6), (7), (8) and (11).

The character of Vǫggr as Hrólfr's avenger is also present in (7), (8), (10) and (11).

Hjǫrvarðr also appears as Hrólfr's bane in (4), (6), (9) and (11), Skuld appearing also in all but (9).

It is clear also that at least some of the time these authors are borrowing not from each other, but from accounts circulating independently; one could not construct a reliable stemma for the legend as a whole.[4] Thus, Saxo and *Hrólfs saga* are in substantial agreement over many things—both for instance tell the tale of Hjalti's testing and mutilation of his mistress on the morning of the Last Stand—but if the author of the saga had had Saxo available to him, or *Skjǫldunga saga*, he would not have concluded his version of the vengeance of Vǫggr so ineptly.

John Niles accordingly, having contemplated 'the bewildering variety of stories told about the Skjöldung kings of Lejre', asks himself the

---

[3] Saxo describes the duel between Agnerus and Biarco, but identifies him as the son of Ingellus, as do the *Bjarkarímur*. These latter also identify the Agnarr who recovers the ring with the Agnarr killed by Biarki.

[4] Though there are some indicators. The saga author may have known Snorri's *Skáldskaparmál*, for both have the saying *Litlu verðr Vǫggr feginn*. If, as suggested by Guðbrandur Vigfússon, *vǫggr* was originally a word for 'small child' as well as a name (see Ellis Davidson and Fisher 1979, II 46), then Hrólfr is making an amusing pun on a proverb parallel to our 'Little things please little minds'. Snorri does not complete the story by telling of Vǫggr's vengeance, though the saga author seems to have felt that the story needed completion, see above. See also Valgerður Brynjólfsdóttir 2003, 141–42.

question, 'Was there ever a more or less unitary form of the tale?' or whether the search for one is only 'an exercise in futility' (Niles 2007, 255). He concludes that the attempt is possible, and offers an 'archetypal' version of the story (260–61), going on with an attempt to relate this to the results of the archaeological excavations at Lejre[5]—the great hall built c.550, the second hall built c.680, the signs of a great cremation c. 630–50. What he suggests is that the legend had no real correspondence with past events, but was made up by people living later in the Lejre area, and attempting to explain memories of the first great hall and the great cremation; the legend would then be based on a ruin, or the memory of a ruin.

This is certainly logical, and it fits the evidence of the archaeology and its dating as theories deduced from *Beowulf*, for instance, do not. There are perhaps two objections to it. One is that the original legend must have been a compelling one to circulate so widely and last so long, in which case it is odd that there is no trace or mention of a first version. A poem? A saga? What we have looks arguably more like a scatter of different witnesses to the same events, with different explanations, relationships and even political standpoints creating different stories—which as we know is what happens in the real world, especially if one is relying on oral accounts—with of course a great deal of further and fantastic accretion.

The other objection (to allow *Beowulf* into the discussion for one paragraph) is that one of the things which makes *Beowulf* rather convincing is the poet's unemphatic, even casual delivery of information which makes a good deal of sense. The poet is not much concerned with the Scylding kings, apart from Hroþgar (or Hróarr), a minor figure in all the Scandinavian accounts. But he lets slip that Heoroweard (or Hjǫrvarðr) is himself a Scylding, the son of an elder brother of Hroþgar and Halga of whom Scandinavian tradition knows nothing. He mentions Hreþric also (= Hrærekr? = Hrókr?), not as Hroþgar's enemy but as his son. The situation in *Beowulf* then (I repeat, quite clearly stated but only peripheral to the poem's narrative) is that there are three paternal first cousins, each with an evident claim to the throne once Hroþgar dies, an event expected in the poem before very long—enough in itself to explain Hrólfr's death at Hleiðra at the hands of Hjǫrvarðr, and perhaps the elimination of Hrærekr/Hrókr by Hrólfr. It is again odd that this neat

---

[5] As known in 2007, but see p. 18 above for further discoveries on the Lejre site, these latter as yet not reported in enough detail to be taken into any interpretation.

and plausible explanation (much more credible than the demonic half-sister Skuld) has vanished from Scandinavian memory. Its existence creates something of a dilemma for the 'original legend' theory. Was it not part of the hypothetical *Ur*-legend, but invented separately in England? In which case one has to wonder why anyone bothered. Or does it preserve something which existed in the 'original legend' but was later eliminated from Scandinavian memory as discreditable to Hrólfr? In which case one must ask why a discreditable version was produced in Scandinavia in the first place. It would be a simpler explanation to say that we have two different views of the same event, a pro-Hrólfr one which suppressed or distorted memories of his rivals, and a more neutral one which offered no judgement on the civil war of the Scyldings generally.

Meanwhile, one could argue that the real-life scenario behind the variant legends is this. In the post-Roman era, a time of major transfers of power within Scandinavia as on its borders, a number of royal or sub-royal dynasties were contending for power, associated with tribal groups such as the Danes, Swedes, Gauts, Bards, Jutes, Frisians and even Angles, along no doubt with even smaller groups of which we have little record. These contentions were remembered in different ways by different groups, and the relationships between them were in any case forgotten (as for instance with Fróði and Hálfdan), as was any exact chronology. Names themselves ceased to be recognised, so that Hálfdan, in *Grottasǫngr*, turns into 'the Half-Danes', while conversely 'the Heaþo-Bards' turn into 'Hothbrodus'. What were well-remembered were dramatic incidents,[6] no doubt embellished and embroidered almost as soon as first told: the battle on the ice of Lake Väner, in which (according to *Skjǫldunga saga*, *Skáldskaparmál* and the *Bjarkarímur*) King Hrólfr's champions fought; the enmity between King Hrólfr and King Aðils, or at any rate between Danes and Swedes; the death of great kings and the fall of dynasties.

Most of *Hrólfs saga* of course looks like pure fantasy, with its elf-women, were-bears, miraculous escapes and berserk-quelling champions, while much of what is left looks like the massaging of Danish *amour propre*, with repeated humiliation of the Swedes, and utter defeat in the end transformed into moral victory (as is regularly the case with utter

---

[6] And sometimes words or phrases associated with the incidents, like the pun or proverb suggested in note 1 above, or the verb *svínbeyga*, which seems to have become a favourite (see *Skáldskaparmál*, I 59 and *Vatnsdœla saga* ch. 33).

defeats). Nor could anyone call it a masterpiece of construction. The author's main aim seems to have been to *get everything in* that he had ever heard about; the saga as a whole would probably be improved by the elimination of Hrókr and Svipdagr, and a reduction in the number of berserks, interventions by Queen Yrsa, and humiliations heaped on Aðils.

One could, however, say something similar about *Vǫlsunga saga*. It too contains its doublings and its internal contradictions, while it has even stronger elements of fantasy. Just as Bǫðvarr is the son of a were-bear, so Sigurðr is the son and half-brother of men who are (albeit temporarily) were-wolves. Helgi's elf-woman is more than matched by Brynhildr the valkyrie. However, the existence of central figures from fairy-tale in *Vǫlsunga saga* has not prevented the general recognition that its Nibelungs, if not its Volsungs, were real figures in history. The Gunnarr of the saga (Guþhere in Old English tradition) is the fifth-century King Gundaharius of the *Lex Burgundionum*, the equation confirmed by the names of other members of his family, Giúki and Giselher corresponding to the Gibica and Gislaharius of the Latin text.[7] In just the same way, Hrólfr in Old Norse and Hroþulf in Old English (their identity confirmed by their family trees) look like descendants of a sixth-century *Hrothuwulfaz, though this time we have no contemporary Latin text to bear witness. It is only this, however, which prevents the drawing of a complete parallel, in which, just as *Vǫlsunga saga* and its analogues preserve memory of the traumatic fifth-century defeat of the Burgundians on the Rhine by the Huns, so *Hrólfs saga* and its analogues would preserve memory of sixth-century events, no doubt equally traumatic, but confined to pre-literate Scandinavia and so not confirmed by contemporary documents. Both sagas, then, could be seen as ripples of events once as real as those which gave us the Atli of the Eddic poems (Old English Ætla, Latin / Gothic Attila), or Iǫrmunrekkr (Old English Eormenrice, Latin Ermanaricus, Gothic *Airmanareiks). One cannot tell how far bearing witness to these may have formed part of their authors' motivation, but preserving the past, and gathering up every possible scrap

---

[7] Christopher Tolkien has recently pointed out (Tolkien 2009, 228) that both Old Norse and Old English poetic tradition quite correctly preserved the memory of the ethnicity of these heroes—which must surely have been forgotten in the wider world—by their use of the phrase for Gunnarr / Guþhere, respectively *vin Borgunda* / *wine Burgenda* 'friend (i.e. lord) of the Burgundians'.

of fading tradition, were certainly strong elements (as well as telling entertaining stories) in the motivation of many if not most medieval Icelandic authors.

Bibliography

Ármann Jakobsson 2003. 'Queens of Terror, Perilous women in *Hálfs saga* and *Hrólfs saga kraka*'. In *Fornaldarsagornas Struktur och Ideologi, Handlingar från ett symposium i Uppsala 31.8–2.9. 2000*. Ed. Ármann Jakobsson et al., 173—89.

Bugge, Sophus 1867. *Norrœn fornkvæði . . . Sæmundar Edda hins fróða*.

Byock, Jesse, trans., 1998. *The Saga of King Hrolf Kraki*.

Christensen, Tom 1991. 'Lejre, Fact and Fable'. Trans. Faith Ingwersen. In *Beowulf and Lejre* 2007. Ed. John D. Niles, 13–101.

Christensen, Tom 2005. 'A New Round of Excavations at Lejre (to 2005)'. Trans. Faith Ingwersen. In *Beowulf and Lejre* 2007. Ed. John D. Niles, 109–26.

Driscoll, M. J. and Silvia Hufnagel 2009. 'Fornaldarsögur norðurlanda: A bibliography of manuscripts, editions, translations and secondary literature'. www.staff.hum.ku.dk/mjd/fornaldarsagas

Ellis Davidson, Hilda, ed., and Peter Fisher, trans., 1979–80. *Saxo Grammaticus. The History of the Danes, Books I–IX*.

Evans, Jonathan 1993. 'Hrólfs saga kraka'. In *Medieval Scandinavia: An Encyclopedia*. Ed. Phillip Pulsiano et al., 304–05.

Fulk, R. D., Robert E. Bjork and John D. Niles, eds., 2008. *Klaeber's Beowulf, 4th Edition*.

Garmonsway, G. N., Jacqueline Simpson and Hilda Ellis Davidson, trans., 1968. *Beowulf and its Analogues*.

Gordon, E.V., ed., 1962. *An Introduction to Old Norse*, 2nd ed. revised by A. R. Taylor.

Hrólfs saga kraka ok kappa hans. In *Fornaldarsögur Norðurlanda* 1954, I–IV. Ed. Guðni Jónsson. I 1–105.

Jones, Gwyn, trans., 1961. *Eirik the Red and other Icelandic Sagas*.

Jones, Gwyn 1968. *A History of the Vikings*.

Kalinke, Marianne 2003. 'Transgression in *Hrólfs saga kraka*'. In *Fornaldarsagornas struktur och ideologi: Handlingar från ett symposium i Uppsala 31.8–2.9. 2000*. Ed. Ármann Jakobsson et al, 157–71.

Koch, John T., ed., 1997. *The Gododdin of Aneirin, Text and Context from Dark-Age Britain*.

Niles, John D., ed., 2007. *Beowulf and Lejre*.

Slay, Desmond, ed., 1960. *Hrólfs saga kraka*. Editiones Arnamagnæanæ B / 1.

Snorri Sturluson 1998. *Skáldskaparmál*. Ed. Anthony Faulkes.

Tolkien, J. R. R. 2009. *The Legend of Sigurd and Gudrún*. Ed. Christopher Tolkien.

Tolley, Clive 2007. '*Hrólfs saga kraka* and Sami bear rites'. *Saga-Book* XXXI, 5–21.

Tunstall, Peter 2003. *The Saga of King Hrolf Kraki and his Champions.* www.northvegr.org/lore/oldheathen/034.php

Valgerður Brynjólfsdóttir 2003. 'A Valiant King or a Coward? The Changing Image of King Hrólfr kraki from the Oldest Sources to *Hrólfs saga kraka*'. In *Fornaldarsagornas struktur och ideologi, Handlingar från ett symposium i Uppsala 31.8–2.9. 2000.* Ed. Ármann Jakobsson et al., 141–56.

ENTER THE DRAGON. LEGENDARY SAGA COURAGE AND THE BIRTH OF THE HERO

ÁRMANN JAKOBSSON

The uses of monsters

'*Þat sagðir þú, Reginn, at dreki sjá væri eigi meiri en einn lyngormr, en mér sýnask vegar hans æfar miklir*' "You claimed, Reginn, that this dragon was no bigger than a regular worm, but he seems to me to leave a mighty track" (*Vǫlsunga saga*, 41).[1] Before killing Fáfnir, Sigurðr Fáfnisbani is far from enthusiastic. Presumably he is not supposed to realise at this point that he will be famous ever after for slaying this dragon, as his nickname attests.[2] According to *Vǫlsunga saga*, he mainly desires revenge for the death of his father; it is his foster-father Reginn who keeps urging him to kill the dragon and he continues to postpone it until he has avenged his kinsmen.

Sigurðr's reluctance is not explained in the saga. If it had been someone else, one might suspect anxiety about confronting the dragon. But as will be discussed in more detail later, it is stated on more than one occasion in *Vǫlsunga saga* that Sigurðr knows no fear. So the most likely option is that he is simply not very interested in the dragon at this stage; he fights it because he has promised to, or so the saga has it: '*Efna munu vér þat sem vér hǫfum þar um heitit, ok ekki fellr oss þat ór minni*' "We will make good on what we have promised, and it has not slipped our mind" (41).

What is the dragon to Sigurðr? His attitude is interestingly nonchalant. The question arises, Who is Sigurðr the dragon-slayer? Why is he the best person to kill the dragon? And furthermore, why is the dragon important to the hero? The subject of this study is the significance of the dragon in a narrative such as the Sigurðr legend, of which *Vǫlsunga saga* is but one of many manifestations.

---

[1] All references to *Vǫlsunga saga* and *Ragnars saga* will be to Olsen's 1906–08 edition. The spelling has been normalised for the sake of clarity.

[2] The nickname *Fáfnisbani* appears three times in *Vǫlsunga saga* (85, 105 and 108). It is also used in other medieval texts such as *Ragnars saga loðbrókar*, Flateyjarbók (in *Norna-Gests þáttr* and *Þorsteins þáttr skelks*) and in *Snorra Edda* (*Skáldskaparmál*). Thus Sigurðr and the dragon seem to be intertwined in the mind of the medieval audience.

The dragon provides the Sigurðr legend with its core. Thus understanding the legend means understanding the meaning dragons held for the contemporary audience of the saga. The idea that a mythical beast such as a dragon might have a symbolic significance would not have been alien to the late medieval audience of *Vǫlsunga saga*. In the Old Icelandic bestiary *Physiologus* (1889), which probably dates from the beginning of the thirteenth century, it is clearly stated that every beast has a symbolic value and serves a particular purpose. This is not surprising in itself since the person or persons responsible for this text believed that the world was created by an omniscient being with a clear design. And even though the natural sciences no longer work from this premise, one can contend that while natural animals may not necessarily be imbued with a divine significance, mythical beasts must always have a function, a symbolic meaning and a narrative purpose, and this certainly applies to dragons.

Meaning and purpose are complicated concepts that need to be defined more closely. This article is concerned with the purpose of the narrative and the practical function of the monster in it, but there is also the possibility that it has a religious purpose, a function within the Christian faith that will not be discussed here but has been noted by other scholars (see e.g. Ásdís Egilsdóttir 1999, Riches 2003). Last but not least, there is the function of a dragon for an implied Everyman within the audience of the saga. Since mythical beasts belong to an 'Otherworld', their function in daily life is far from obvious from the perspective of the twenty-first century. But I believe this function is both real and important; that it is in fact the spinal cord of the legend.

One of the problematic aspects of the dragon-slaying myth is how to approach it. There are several medieval texts about Sigurðr Fáfnisbani, pictures as well as narratives, but there is also the legend—a different kind of text—which materialises in texts including *Vǫlsunga saga*, which will be the focus of this study. The scholar who wishes to say something about the heroic dragon-slayer myth is trying to interpret an intangible text which does not exist on paper; it is necessary to work from versions of it in narratives such as the legendary sagas and use them as a pathway to the essence of the myth.

There are two good reasons for this. One is that myths and legends always express themselves through language and thus there is no clear separation between beliefs or ideas and their linguistic expression.[3] The

---

[3] I see no reason to distinguish between myths and legends in this study. Demarcation between the two is far from clear and definitions vary. Bascom (1965) defines myths as having non-human principal characters and as belonging to the

second is my interest in the practical uses and functions of myths for an imagined audience, in this case thirteenth-, fourteenth- and fifteenth-century Icelanders, the audience of *Reginsmál, Fáfnismál, Vǫlsunga saga* and *Ragnars saga loðbrókar*. Thus it seems logical to approach the myth as they did, through the text of a legendary saga, a text which retells a legend although its form is its own.[4]

The troublesome relationship between the legend and its existing textual variants cannot really be resolved. In this study, no attempt will be made to decapitate this hydra or even look it in the eye; rather I will approach it tentatively, as might an unnamed and unheroic supporting character in a dragon-slaying myth. *Vǫlsunga saga* and *Ragnars saga* will be the texts that I cling to, knowing that they are only fragments of a much larger and somewhat nebulous vessel lurking in the deep. In this analogy, the philologist is adrift in the ocean and myths can indeed be as vast and as complex (or as simple) as an ocean.

What kind of text is a legend or a myth? There is no shortage of definitions, and trying not to get completely lost at sea, I will concentrate on the functionality of myths and legends (to me perhaps their most interesting side), since this is the aspect of the myth lost to a modern audience that does not believe in the myth and starts out impervious to its possible explanatory value. Modern scholars tend not to regard stories such as *Vǫlsunga saga* as 'practical literature' and thus they may miss some of its value to its original audience.[5]

---

ancient past, whereas legends are closer in time and do have human principal characters. This definition has been criticised by Csapo (2005, 3–9) who questions the need for such a clear demarcation. To clarify my stance, I understand 'legend' as a traditional narrative, not necessarily historically accurate (though purporting to be). 'Myth', on the other hand, I would use mainly about cosmological narratives with an explanatory function. However, it could be argued that legends serve a similar function, although less overtly, and the difference between the two is thus not very real. As I understand it, both the Sigurðr and the Ragnarr legends are a part of a larger unity which is really a myth, that of the dragon-slaying youth.

[4] Various views on the troublesome relationship between tradition and form in the legendary sagas can be seen in 'Interrogating genre in the fornaldarsögur: Round-table discussion' (2006). One thing which is clear from this discussion is that the legendary sagas can be approached both as a part of a long tradition and as singular works with their own structure, style and ideology which is not necessarily an integral part of the original legend.

[5] As Hastrup (1987, 261) has noted, history has an explanatory function not unlike that of myth; both are 'selective accounts of the past', concerned with the creation of identity and the establishment of precedent. The main difference lies

But the functionality and the meaning of a myth—in this case there is no real need to distinguish between the two since I am looking at the meaning of the myth from the perspective of an audience that wants to put it to some use—is a complex matter.[6] The functionality of myths means that a myth always exists in two time zones: on one hand, in the very ancient past where it has been placed, and on the other, right in the middle of the present, in the lives of its audience (see e.g. Hastrup 1987, 259). The myth is very distant, as all deities and venerated figures have to be. And yet the myth exists within ourselves and thus everywhere. Myths can be quite complex but at the same time their essence tends to be very simple, even mundane. Myths are supposed to explain the world and invent a harmony between the inner and the outer, the vast and the small, thus helping a simple human, in his smallness, to grasp a complex world. Since life is not static, neither are myths. They are narratives on the move, perhaps in the form of a quest, with a clear purpose that is often absent from our everyday lives and where the hard struggle of the hero provides the myth with an intensity that we may sometimes lack in our daily existence.

Thus myths are paradoxical; they have to be lofty and cosmological, explaining the biggest things imaginable to men (god, the sky, time, life), but they also act as a guide to the small and insignificant private lives of ordinary people. If myths and legends did not address the ordinariness of existence, they would lose much of their power. And this is what I am approaching here: the meaning that an extraordinary hero such as Sigurðr and a huge, mythical beast such as a dragon holds in the trivial existence of, say, poor farmers and their families in the peaceful Icelandic countryside.

Since the Sigurðr myth is ubiquitous, as myths should perhaps aspire to be, it assumes that there is a Sigurðr inside every man and the legend thus has a function for everyone. But it also has to be kept in mind that Sigurðr is a king as well, and it is also an important function of the legend to sustain the charisma of leadership and the qualities of a noble ruler.[7] The legendary past is always two-dimensional: it concerns both society

in the orality and timelessness of myths, whereas history is literary and more firmly grounded in time.

[6] There are many far more subtle and nuanced definitions of myths than are possible in this limited study. See esp. Schjødt 2008, 64–68, who emphasises the legitimising function of myth.

[7] I have written at greater length about the myth of kingship/leadership in the medieval North (Ármann Jakobsson 1997, 89–154).

and the life of the individual. But most importantly, the mythical hero is gone but still present; the legend is not just storytelling about the past but also an afterlife for the hero who continues to serve his didactic function, and this hero matters to the everyday lives of his audience and is far more intimate than he later became.

I will focus on the personal rather than the public function of the legend although I think it can be argued that it had practical value for its West Nordic audience as an analysis of society as well as of the psychology of the individual. My main subject will be how the legend expresses, but also to a degree problematises, the concepts of youth and courage, through the figures of the hero and the dragon. I will discuss how dragons serve both as the midwives of heroism (and this analogy is not out of the blue) and as the embodiment of terror. While dragons are not a part of the daily existence of most people, fear most certainly is, and I will argue here that fear is one of the cornerstones of heroism and that terror imbues the most important Old Norse dragon legends with a clear purpose.

A hierarchy of serpents

In the heroic North, dragon-slayers seem to have been in a heroic class of their own, a class with only two members (or three if we count Beowulf). These are Sigurðr Fáfnisbani and Ragnarr loðbrók. The dragons killed by Sigurðr and Ragnarr are not the only two that are slain in the medieval Norse-Icelandic textual corpus; indeed, there are several serpents of various types to be found there. And yet Ragnarr and Sigurðr seem to have stood out among Northern European dragon-slayers, especially Sigurðr who may well be regarded as the principal dragon-slayer of the North, the Germanic exemplar of the dragon-slaying myth that Calvert Watkins (1995, 297–303) has located throughout the Indo-European world.

In Old Icelandic texts the word *dreki* often denotes an animal of far lesser stature than those fought by Sigurðr and Ragnarr. J. R. R. Tolkien may have exaggerated when he said that in the North, dragons were 'as rare as they are dire' (Tolkien 1936, 253; see Evans 2005, 241–48 for counter-examples), but he was right that it is necessary to distinguish between really impressive and less frightening dragons. The *flugdrekar* that Gull-Þórir and his companions slay in *Þorskfirðinga saga* (185–88) when stealing their hoard command so little respect that they can hardly be referred to in the same breath as Fáfnir. These dragons are so large that they can carry a man in their jaws, and they also fly and spew fire and poison, yet the narrative is devoid of any sense of wonder or danger.[8] The dragon that Bjǫrn Hítdœlakappi slays in his saga hardly seems worth a mention, either in this study or indeed in *Bjarnar saga Hítdœlakappa* itself, where it is referred to very perfunctorily—and after its slaying, never mentioned again (*Bjarnar saga Hítdœlakappa*, 124); and although Þorkell the bully in *Njáls saga* boasts of having killed another *flugdreki*, he is put in his place by Skarphéðinn: killing a dragon does not seem to compare with the heroism of skating over a frozen river to kill a chieftain in his sixties accompanied by seven people, including youths, farmhands and women (*Brennu-Njáls saga*, 303).[9] And even though Haraldr harðráði's mettle is certainly put to the test when making short work of the emperor of Constantinople's dungeon dragon (a type of monster familiar to anyone who has seen the film *The Return of the Jedi*) in Saxo's *Gesta Danorum* (10) and *Morkinskinna* (80–82), he emerges from the pit an unchanged man. His dragon is admittedly terrible but not the making of the man. So I would tend to agree with Tolkien that not all dragons are equally magnificent, and that the dragon-slayings of Sigurðr Fáfnisbani and Ragnarr are the only clear Old Norse representations of the powerful dragon-slaying myth.[10] In this instance the word *dreki* may not be the best guide to the *draconitas* of Sigurðr and Ragnarr's antagonists.[11]

The two slayers of NKS 1824b 4to

The dragon killed by Bjǫrn Hítdœlakappi earns him no special status in the Mýrasýsla district in Iceland. On the other hand, Sigurðr Fáfnisbani and Ragnarr loðbrók are two of the most celebrated heroic figures of the medie-

---

[8] This lack of a sense of wonder or danger may perhaps be regarded as typical of this saga type, see Sävborg 2009. At the end of the saga, it is suggested in an equally offhand fashion that Þórir himself may have changed into a dragon instead of dying (*Þorskfirðinga saga*, 226).

[9] According to the saga, Þorkell has also fought a *finngálkn* 'chimera'.

[10] Not all monster-fighters are dragon-slayers and there are some heroic figures in the Old Icelandic sagas that fight ghosts, trolls, and berserkers. Grettir Ásmundarson is perhaps the most 'professional' of these monster-fighters (see for example Ármann Jakobsson 2009) but one might also mention the *Hrafnistumenn* (Ciklamini 1966), the family of Bárðr Snæfellsáss (Ármann Jakobsson 1998), heroes who wrestle with *blámenn*, and grave-robbing episodes in howes (Ármann Jakobsson 2010) where there is usually a ghost or two to guard the treasure sought.

[11] The word is not Germanic but Greek (see for example Evans 2005, 217), and, as it indicates, there is no clear separation between the Germanic dragon and its Indo-European counterparts (Evans, 221–30).

val North. Ragnarr pales in comparison to Sigurðr, yet his dragon-slaying is not only included in the subject matter of *Ragnars saga loðbrókar* but also referred to in several other Old Norse texts: *Hervarar saga ok Heiðreks*, *Bósa saga ok Herrauðs*, *Hálfdanar saga Eysteinssonar* and *Norna-Gests þáttr*. He also figures in Saxo's *Gesta Danorum* and in *Hauksbók*. As Rory McTurk (1991) has demonstrated, the Ragnarr tradition is old and wide-ranging.[12]

Sigurðr, of course, is even more distinguished. He makes appearances all over the Germanic world, in the *Nibelungenlied*,[13] in *Beowulf*,[14] in images carved on Swedish runestones and in several Old Norse texts, including *Snorra Edda*, *Þiðreks saga* and *Vǫlsunga saga* (see e.g. Andersson 1980; Rowe 2006). His story is worthy of being retold at length in the Codex Regius of the Elder Edda, alongside mythical texts such as *Vǫluspá*, *Hávamál* and *Vafþrúðnismál*, and he even makes it into the late fourteenth-century *Þorsteins þáttr skelks* in Flateyjarbók as a prime example of a heroic heathen, before becoming the hero of several post-medieval ballads in various parts of Scandinavia.

Þorsteins þáttr is worth special consideration because in this late narrative Sigurðr has exemplary and didactic value but is no longer an unproblematic hero; according to the ghostly demon Þorkell þunni, he is serving in Hell along with other heathen warriors, including Starkaðr the Old (*Flateyjarbok*, 416). In the formalist narrative research of the 1960s it became customary to distinguish between two types of heroes, the bright and beautiful hero and the somewhat darker and more problematic one. Lars Lönnroth (1976, 62) called these two types the Grettir-type and the Siegfried-type, so it is clear where Sigurðr Fáfnisbani fits in, and the crimes that Starkaðr commits mark him down equally obviously as the Grettir-type (see e.g. Ciklamini 1971). In *Þorsteins þáttr* both types are represented, and there is clearly a difference: Sigurðr bears his hellish punishment with fortitude while Starkaðr reacts with inhuman howling. But the difference proves on closer inspection to be superficial: in spite of Starkaðr's harsher punishment and Sigurðr's fortitude, both are heathen and in the same Hell.

Þorsteins þáttr skelks is preserved in Flateyjarbók, which presents its audience with a rigorously Augustinian world view where the heathen past

---

[12] McTurk uses eighteen narratives, including Renaissance Latin accounts and ballads, presumably post-medieval, from Denmark, Norway and the Faroe Islands to analyse the pattern of the Ragnarr and Áslaug part of *Ragnars saga* (McTurk 1991, 53–62).

[13] In the *Nibelungenlied* Sigurðr is given the name Sifrit (Siegfried).

[14] In *Beowulf* (ll. 875–892) the dragon-slaying is credited to Sigemund, who in Norse versions (as Sigmundr) is the father of Sigurðr.

is clearly placed in Hell (see Rowe 2005, 65–97). But who is Sigurðr? Why is his legend so popular and what is its function? Why does the late fourteenth-century editorial team of Flateyjarbók care about this prehistoric heroic figure? As clearly portrayed in *Ragnars saga*, Sigurðr acquires some significance as the mythical ancestor of the perhaps equally mythical King Haraldr hárfagri of Norway and the northern kings descended in his line.[15] That is, however, hardly enough in itself to explain his elevated status within the culture of medieval Scandinavia. It seems more likely that his importance lies in the dragon-slaying itself, in myth rather than history, a quality which also manages to elevate Ragnarr loðbrók over most other prehistoric Viking kings, although perhaps not quite to the same heights as Sigurðr.

Ragnarr is actually Sigurðr's son-in-law according to *Ragnars saga*, but the two heroes do not have much in common apart from the dragon-slaying. And there are also significant differences in the most detailed narratives of the two killings. With Ragnarr, the emphasis is on his ingenuity and mainly on the hairy breeches which he uses to escape the poison of the worm and which provide him with a lasting identity, whereas in the Sigurðr narrative, the emphasis is on his desire for revenge and the influence from Reginn. Still, there are some shared elements worthy of interest. We find evidence for this in the legendary saga variations of the myth, in *Vǫlsunga saga* and *Ragnars saga*, composed presumably separately in the thirteenth or early fourteenth century but preserved together in the early fifteenth-century manuscript NKS 1824 b 4to.[16] I use these texts as representatives for the myth in this paper, not because they are the oldest or the most original variants but because they demonstrate the possible functions of the myth for a late medieval audience who encountered it through these texts.

[15] As evidenced by the manuscript AM 415 4to from the early fourteenth century, where also Ragnarr is the purported ancestor of the kings of Denmark, Norway and Sweden (on this manuscript, see Sverrir Jakobsson 2005, 50).

[16] The text in 1824 is not believed to be necessarily close to the presumed original version of either saga (on the relationship between the extant *Vǫlsunga saga* and other narratives of Sigurðr and Brynhildr, see esp. Andersson 1980; on the development of the Ragnarr narratives, see McTurk 1991). If *Vǫlsunga saga* dates from the thirteenth century as e.g. Andersson (1999) believes, the narrative may have evolved quite a bit before the extant version was committed to paper. Nevertheless, 1824 is the only existing vellum manuscript of *Vǫlsunga saga* and the only complete one of *Ragnars saga* (Olsen also published the fragmentary AM 147 4to in his 1906 edition). At least twenty-one paper manuscripts containing both sagas are believed to date back to this manuscript (Olsen, vii–x).

Youth and the hero

As seen above, the Sigurðr we meet in *Vǫlsunga saga* is not at first particularly interested in fighting the dragon Fáfnir. He treats Reginn's persistence in the matter as a teenage boy might treat his mother's insistence that he clean his room. His main desire is to avenge his father but the saga insists that he also wants to keep his promise to Reginn. The saga keeps reminding us that Sigurðr knows no fear (see below), and if we take that at face value, his initial reluctance to fight the dragon has to be interpreted not as a lack of courage but rather as lack of interest. Even though he claims to have heard of Fáfnir (33), his youthful carelessness highlights his status at this point in the saga as a callow boy who does not acknowledge that fighting a dragon is the most heroic achievement imaginable.

One thing that the dragon-slayers of *Vǫlsunga saga* and *Ragnars saga* do have in common is that both heroes are youths. When Reginn has started goading Sigurðr to kill the dragon, Sigurðr remarks that he is 'still little more than a child' (*vér erum enn lítt af barns aldri*) (33), and it is only a short while later that he avenges his father and then goes on to slay the dragon. His youth is also clear in the ensuing conversation between the dragon and his slayer. Fáfnir calls him '*sveinn*' and keeps asking about his father (42), which annoys Sigurðr no end, as evidenced by his childishly irritable replies.[17]

In *Ragnars saga* Ragnarr claims to be fifteen years of age when he kills the dragon, and the earl's daughter he has liberated finds him more like an ogre than a man of such a young age: *þykkisk hon eigi vita, hvárt hann er mennskr maðr eða eigi, fyrir því at henni þykkir vǫxtr hans vera svá mikill sem sagt er frá óvættum á þeim aldri sem hann hafði* 'she seemed not to know whether he was human or not, for his stature seemed to her as big as that of ogres is said to be, considering how old he was' (119).[18] Thus it is an important factor in both stories, at least in their legendary saga form, that the

---

[17] This is even more evident in the version of their conversation in *Fáfnismál* (*Poetic Edda* 180–88, esp. stanzas 1–8 and 12–13). The word *sveinn* implies a certain lack of masculine power, being mainly used about youths and servants; note its effective use by Bjǫrn Hítdœlakappi in the defamatory verses he composes about his rival Þórðr (*Bjarnar saga Hítdœlakappa*, 140–44).

[18] Whether from the shock of seeing this monster-like teenager or not, she then goes into her hut and promptly falls asleep (*ok snýr hún inn í skemmuna ok sofnar*) (119). Compare Larrington's interpretation of the king-princess-dragon triangle in this volume (pp. 58–60).

hero is young, indeed still a teenager, a man between childhood and adulthood.[19]

The youth of the hero means that the climactic event of his life is placed early in the narrative. What happens after the dragon-slaying may be one long decline. Although it can be disputed whether the two heroes are failures in later life, it can at least be stated fairly that neither of them ever accomplishes anything similar to the dragon-slaying. Both continue to be brave men, in their death as well as their life, but Sigurðr gets entangled in a marriage quadrangle with Gunnarr, Guðrún and Brynhildr and is killed at a young age. Ragnarr loðbrók survives but ends up going on a disastrous expedition to England in his old age in a vain attempt to gain fame equal to that which his sons now possess (154).

But how do we explain this emphasis on the youth of the dragon-slayer? To address that question, it is necessary to go on to the second common denominator of the Sigurðr and Ragnarr narratives: the bravery that the hero needs to confront the worm.

Fear is the key

When Siguðr finally sees Fáfnir, the dragon seems impressive but hardly enough to scare Sigurðr, as the saga says (42):

> Ok er ormrinn skreið til vatns varð mikill landskjálfti, svá at ǫll jǫrð skalf í nánd. Hann fnýsti eitri alla leið fyrir sik fram, ok eigi hræddisk Sigurðr né óttask við þann gný.
>
> And when the worm crawled to water there was a great earthquake so that all the ground in the vicinity moved. He spewed poison everywhere in front of him, and Sigurðr was not afraid and did not fear this noise.

The saga's insistence on Sigurðr's absence of fear (repeated in the synonyms *hræddisk* and *óttask*) emphasises that fear is exactly what is to be expected in this situation—lying in a ditch awaiting the arrival of a gigantic and poisonous, not to mention noisy, reptile.

In *Ragnars saga*, fear also seems to be the key element of the *draconitas* of the worm. When the worm that dwells on Þóra's casket begins to grow, people become terrified of it (*Þorir engi maðr at koma til skemmunnar fyrir þessum ormi* 'No one dared to come to the chamber because of the serpent') (117), making her a virtual recluse. Fear is the problem that Ragnarr needs to solve: it is the people's fear of this serpent which has isolated Þóra. So fear as a major theme in the dragon-slaying legend

---

[19] This makes perfect sense if the myth is seen as an initiation ritual (Schjødt 1994; on initiation rituals, see further Eliade 1974, 17–18).

is present in *Ragnars saga* as it is also from the beginning of that part of *Vǫlsunga saga*. When Fáfnir the dragon is first mentioned Sigurðr, somewhat pompously using the plural form *vér*, remarks: '*Kann ek kyn þessa orms, þótt vér séim ungir, ok hefi ek spurt, at engi þorir at koma á mót honum fyrir vaxtar sakar ok illsku*' "I know the nature of this worm even though we are young, and I have heard that nobody dares to face it on account of its size and evil" (33).

When Reginn has extracted from Sigurðr a promise to kill the dragon, he keeps expressing doubts that Sigurðr will make it good, and when they have come to the heath where Fáfnir dwells he starts goading his young apprentice again: '*Eigi má þér ráð ráða, er þú ert við hvatvetna hræddr*' "I cannot advise you if you fear everything" (41). The text is full of talk of fear, and this is no accident; fear is indeed the key to the understanding of these two dragons. What they have in common is the fear they inspire in others.

To return to the symbolism of the dragon in the dragon-slaying myth, both dragons may be said to represent, even embody, terror, and in *Vǫlsunga saga* this terror is somewhat over-obviously symbolised by the Helmet of Fear (the *ægishjálmr*) that Fáfnir possesses. As the dragon remarks in *Vǫlsunga saga*, '*Hafðir þú eigi frétt þat, hversu allt fólk er hrætt við mik ok við minn ægishjálm?*' "Had you not heard how everyone is afraid of me and my Helmet of Fear?" (42). The dragon seems almost vexed that the young hero is not suitably scared by him, but the Helmet of Fear is presumably a powerful tool to oppress anyone and anything that comes in his way, the Gnitaheiði version of a Death Star. In *Fáfnismál* the *ægishjálmr* is unexplained and may be metaphorical (as it still is in modern Icelandic, see Jón Friðjónsson 1993, 736); we note a change in *Vǫlsunga saga* to a literal Helmet of Fear that Sigurðr can carry away with him, along with a golden byrnie and the sword Hrotti (47), but what does not change is the symbolic meaning of the helmet. The dragon has a Helmet of Fear because, put simply, it is terror itself. It rules by fear, just as much as by power and poison.

Thus the dragon is far from being mere beast; Tolkien, in his time, warned the scholar indirectly against approaching dragons 'as a sober zoologist' (Tolkien 1936, 11). Instead a dragon is a hybrid of several actual animals, with its wings and its scales, its claws and its serpent-like length—along with the terrible fire that it breathes (in the preserved *Vǫlsunga saga* (42) the emphasis is actually more on its venom), which belongs not to the animal kingdom but to the human mind, from our fear of the destructive power of fire, well-known to humans, one assumes, from the day our race first tried to master it. As *Vǫlsunga saga* clearly indicates, a dragon is also poisonous and has magical powers, two attributes greatly feared in the Middle Ages. Perhaps it is its magic that should be feared most, as is tentatively suggested in *Fáfnismál*, but in *Vǫlsunga saga* the threat is somewhat unspecified. One might even wonder if the words of President Roosevelt might not be applicable, that what one should fear when facing a dragon is fear itself or rather its paralysing effect. The repetition in *Vǫlsunga saga* of Sigurðr's absence of fear at the very moment he encounters the dragon is at least noteworthy.[20]

The reason why fear is referred to in both *Vǫlsunga saga* and *Ragnars saga*, immediately before the young hero accomplishes his feat, and why a dragon should possess a Helmet of Fear that causes all to cower (although it is not really explained in the saga why a gigantic fire-spewing serpent needs a gadget for people to be afraid of it) thus seems to be that fear (symbolised by the helmet) is the dragon's most powerful tool, far more powerful than any poison, fire or brute force.

In his useful article on Germanic dragons, Jonathan Evans does not discuss at length the fear symbolised by the dragon, arguing instead that it represents greed (Evans 2005, 261–69).[21] It is true that in both these legends (the Sigurðr legend and the Ragnarr legend) there is a clear connection between dragons and gold and thus with greed, both the dragon's own greed and that of others. In *Vǫlsunga saga* and *Ragnars saga*, though, fear is accentuated much more strongly. Although desire for gold may be a motivation for Reginn, desire for vengeance is more prominently voiced (37 and 41), and gold seems to provide no motivation for Sigurðr Fáfnisbani, although he takes Fáfnir's gold when he sees it. It is quite unclear what possesses Ragnarr to fight his dragon; although he ends up in deep mourning for Þóra, he has never seen her before the fight, and thus it seems more logical that his motivation is heroism for its own sake, since the key fact in the narrative preceding the killing seems to be the terrifying nature of the worm that nobody dares to approach.

A dragon can, of course, be seen as an embodiment both of its own savage greed and of others' fear.[22] I would contend that for the youthful

[20] Beowulf is also said to be unafraid before fighting his dragon (ll. 2345–50).

[21] As he puts it: 'the key to the dragon's mythic function lies in its narrative role . . . as a monstrous double of its human opponents and, more specifically, as a symbolic mirror of the monstrous transformations wrought upon the human personality through the effects of avarice' (209).

[22] As Cohen notes (1996, 4): 'The monster's body quite literally incorporates fear, desire, anxiety, and fantasy (ataractic or incendiary), giving them life and an uncanny independence.'

hero, the first is not very important but the second all-important. When Sigurðr has killed the dragon, *Vǫlsunga saga* describes him with loving attention to detail, his armour and his weapons, his gracious manners, his chestnut hair and curls, his sharp eyes and his powerful shoulders. And it ends with this statement: *Eigi skorti hann hug ok aldri varð hann hræddr* 'He did not lack courage and he was never afraid' (57). If the dragon is first and foremost an embodiment of terror, in that the fears of the audience are projected onto him, it is equally clear that this is why Sigurðr defeats it, and why it is so important that he is not afraid when the dragon slides over him. For the fearless youth, fear does not exist and thus it can be vanquished. In this myth, overcoming the fear of the dragon means its automatic destruction.

It is fitting that Sigurðr should later make an appearance in *Þorsteins þáttr skelks* which may be regarded as a late fourteenth-century adaption of the folktale 'The Boy Who Knew No Fear' (AT 326) (Aarne/Thompson 1961, 114–15).[23] This is a reminder that there are actually two kinds of fearlessness: one is a handicap, a defect in a young man too simple to know fear, too limited to understand what it is. This is not how Sigurðr's lack of fear is defined; his courage makes him more rather than less of a man.

Eros and courage

Although trying to find a place for dragon-slaying in the lives of ordinary people might at first seem to slight the hero, it is precisely that sort of reference to the ordinary that seems to have attracted a medieval audience to all kinds of sagas. Although Sigurðr is an exceptional figure, his courage is something that everyone in the audience can relate to, since it is composed of people who have known fear and had to rely on courage, although it also seems likely that their relationship with it varied quite a bit.[24] It must also be stressed that fear is a powerful emotion which often expresses itself as a feeling of vulnerability and loss of power. It is quite fundamental to medieval man's identity (see for example Slenczka 2007), certainly in the Old Icelandic society of the Middle Ages, as indeed has been established (see esp. Clover 1993). One may speculate whether this cultural veneration of fear necessarily indicates a great surplus of courage in society. Legends of courage may have been more necessary

---

[23] On the history of this folktale in Iceland, see Lindow 1978.

[24] On the cultural importance and the representations of fear in the Middle Ages, see e.g. Dinzelbacher 1996. The journal *Mittelalter* (first volume of 2007) also contains some interesting studies of the uses of terror in the Middle Ages.

to the medieval man, being more exposed to nature than his modern counterpart.

On a personal level, the legend also concerns the ages of man, an important medieval theme (Burrow 1986). There are all kinds of fear, and indeed many kinds of triumphs over anxiety: existential, moral and physical. The fear of the dragon can be characterised as a strong physical fear in face of supernatural darkness—supernatural danger being especially potent since it is unknown and thus in close union with the feeling of impotence that characterises strong physical fear. The dragon is also intensely physical, an enormity of physicality. It is savage and bestial and its threat is of death itself: a nasty, brutish and short death. It is thus logical that the man who may defeat a dragon should be far removed from death and full of vitality and zest, the life-force that some might call Eros.[25] In fact, the perfect person to conquer this image of death is a youth, a teenager, and our heroes are indeed both in their teens. Thus the dragon can, through its downfall, become a symbol of teenage power.

Sigurðr (somewhat insolently) says to Fáfnir as the latter lies dying: '*Fárr er gamall harðr, ef hann er í bernsku blautr*' "Few are tough in later life if they are cowardly in childhood" (43). Having conquered the dragon, the youth can now nonchalantly regard courage as his own property, and the disregard for physical fear is indeed a well-known characteristic of youth—or at least a part of the myth of youth. Young men are known for not caring about consequences, ignoring danger and braving death in various ways.[26] They often possess great physical courage but are on the other hand given to social fears, things like being unpopular among peers, talking to strangers at parties, being uncool, being the object of scorn.[27] Killing a dragon seems comparatively easy.

---

[25] In Freudian psychology (from Freud's *Beyond the Pleasure Principle* (1920) onwards), it is customary to acknowledge two opposing forces; the life instinct (Eros) and the death instinct (Thanatos), although Freud himself did not use the latter concept (Freud 1973, CPW XVIII). See esp. Marcuse 1972, 35–54 and 142–56.

[26] The death drive, as defined by Freud, is mainly intended to explain behaviour that does not seem to be governed by Eros. It is internal (and does not depend on actual physical danger) and involves repetition and conservative behaviour. While the aggressiveness of youth may take a destructive form, it nevertheless seems logical to perceive it, including the fearlessness and courtship of death, rather as a part of its erotic energy (see e.g. May 1972, 151).

[27] According to Carroll, it is the fear that they will be unable to handle their own emotions that draws modern adolescents to horror films that are able to educate them in the process of emotional management (Carroll 2010, 233–34).

In feudal society such tempestuous youths formed a social group; Georges Duby refers to bands of aristocratic youths in twelfth-century France who formed 'the cutting edge of feudal aggressiveness' (1968, 200). From thirteenth-century Iceland we have the example of the aggressive youthful band, the Þorvaldssynir of Vatnsfjǫrðr, who go to conquer their own dragon, the mighty chieftain Sturla Sighvatsson, but whose spirited attack fails to be heroic since all they encounter instead are women and unarmed men, whom they kill and wound with all the frenzy that might have come in handy against a dragon (*Íslendinga saga* ch. 71; see Ármann Jakobsson 2003).

In our Northern legends of dragon-slayers, the dragon-slaying takes place in the hero's youth and is the climax of the hero's life. It must be added that the dragon in *Beowulf* does not seem at first to fit into the pattern, even though it was approved by Tolkien as a 'real dragon' in his famous essay on *Beowulf*.[28] Beowulf kills the dragon in his old age but does not survive; he is unable to overcome the dragon in the same way as the heroic youths Sigurðr and Ragnarr do. The myth is reversed: Beowulf had earned youthful glory by fighting another kind of monster and then middle-aged glory by being a good king for fifty years. The dragon-slaying is no longer the birth of the hero but rather his end.[29] Not every dragon can be vanquished, and the really successful dragon-slayers are youths.

Youth and fear go hand in hand in the dragon-slaying legends of Sigurðr and Ragnarr. In both instances, the dragon-slaying takes place in the hero's youth and is the climax of the hero's life. The fortitude the hero needs is the fortitude of youth, that zest for life and belief in one's invincibility that leads to disregard for death and fearlessness in face of physical danger, and in both legendary sagas youth and fearlessness are the hero's main attributes. The sagas' versions of the myth reflect a youthful point of view: killing dragons is something one can accomplish but relationships with in-laws are complicated and messy and beyond one's skills.

Uncanny paternity

As a child Sigurðr seems to have no flaws. He is young, he is strong, he is beloved, he is brave and he is truthful (see 31–32). There is no conflict in Sigurðr's life until he has killed the dragon with Reginn's sword. Then the dragon starts talking. Even though Sigurðr has had advice from Reginn and more advice

[28] Somewhat mysteriously, Tolkien does not count the dragon fought by Ragnarr as a proper dragon in his essay.

[29] His companion Wiglaf, the *geong garwiga* who also manages to overcome his fear of the dragon (*Beowulf*, ll 2602–2821), is the survivor instead, after having aided Beowulf in conquering the dragon.

from another unnamed elderly man on the heath, easily identifiable as Óðinn, the audience has had no warning that this might happen and Fáfnir's dialogue is also unexpected. He starts asking Sigurðr who his father is and why he was so bold (*djarfr*) as to strike against the dragon (42). Sigurðr for some reason conceals his name—the reason is given in *Fáfnismál*: he is avoiding the curse of the dying foe (*Poetic Edda*, 180)—but then reveals it. Fáfnir keeps asking him about his father: '*Hver eggjaði þik . . . þú áttir feðr snarpan*' "Who egged you on . . . you had a fierce father" (42) and Sigurðr in turn asks him about the norns (witches) that help mothers give birth to their sons (43).[30]

This interest in midwives and in paternity is striking and perhaps a clue to a further symbolic value of the dragon. As dragon-slaying is a young man's business, the dragon becomes a kind of paternal figure to the dragon-slayer, also in the sense that the dragon (and his death) is the making of the hero. This symbolism is particularly obvious in the case of Fáfnir who is the brother of Reginn, Sigurðr's foster-father. It does not seem so strange that a young man should regard his father's brother, even in dragon shape, as a paternal figure. The conversation between Sigurðr and the dragon revolves around fathers, mothers, sons and midwifes—and fear, the Helmet of Fear which Fáfnir possesses. It is as the embodiment of fear that the dragon is indeed the father of the hero, the hero who conquers the fear (embodied by the dragon) which leaves others paralysed and unheroic.

The dragon, the supernatural unknown, thus is not quite as unknown as it might seem at first sight. However, the sudden realisation of the parental status of the dragon that accompanies the civilised (and yet far from innocent) conversation of the monster and its bane raises new questions and worries.[31] The conversation between the dragon and the hero and the intellectual game they play moves the dragon from one monster category to another and thus brings the monster closer to the hero.

One might say that monsters would at first sight seem to fall roughly into two categories. There is, on the one hand, the monster which is the complete Other and for which no affinity with man seems possible, a monster that is more beast than man. Many monsters initially appear to belong to

---

[30] As Ásdís Egilsdóttir (1999) has demonstrated, the function of the dragon in imagery of birth is not limited to the Germanic tradition.

[31] More than a quarter of a decade ago at least one eleven-year old Reykjavík schoolboy was shocked and repelled to hear a scary monster in its heavy futuristic armour claim to be the father of the baby-faced protagonist of *The Empire Strikes Back* (1980). But the father-and-son relationship of ogre and hero was a well-grounded part of the pervasive mediaevalism of *Star Wars*, George Lucas's enormously successful six-part space blockbuster.

this type, although perhaps wrongly, since animals in literature are never wholly similar to and never entirely different from humans (Riches 2003, 199). The other type is the monster as our double: the human monster, and all speaking monsters belong in some way to this category. The same would seem to apply to most Old Icelandic monsters, such as the Eddic giants, who are not only the gods' main antagonists but also their ancestors and relations by marriage, and shapeshifters, a well-known category of medieval monsters, which includes werewolves and, perhaps, berserkers. Once Sigurðr and Fáfnir start talking, we are reminded of Fáfnir's human origins (see also Evans 2005, 250–56). He is a shapeshifter as well, a man turned into a dragon, and thus is not as utterly alien as he seemed at first.

The dragon is no longer merely terrible and bestial, something that is utterly alien to the human hero, he now also becomes uncanny, strange and yet familiar, human and yet not human,[32] acting almost as if he is Sigurðr's parent and teacher and not merely a monster in the wilderness, though the dialogue does concern his monstrosity and the danger he poses. Nicholas Royle (2003, 1) has said that the 'uncanny involves feelings of uncertainty, in particular regarding the reality of who one is and what is being experienced'. These are feelings of uncertainty which a young man might have who has just killed a beast and now has to have a conversation with it and remember that the beast is actually the brother of his foster-father.[33]

An uncanny relationship is established between the hero and the dragon, who in a sense becomes the hero's double: the evil ancestor the hero has to fight, and who is a part of him, indeed the key to his being, and yet also the main threat to his existence. Every father figure is also a symbol of the past and of death. The first is not so hard to argue: of course your ancestor is the past. Death is the stowaway passenger that invariably goes with the past, and, as the past is the time that has vanished, it must also signify one's own passing. Each generation, occupying the place that the next generation will then fill, must serve as a reminder of the mutability of existence. The decline of one's parents is a terrifying signal to oneself that as one generation passes away, so must the next.

---

[32] In his 1919 essay Freud defines the uncanny as that which is familiar and yet strange, thus frightening (Freud 1973, 220). As Royle (2003) has shown, Freud's depiction of the uncanny is complex and full of ambiguities. Royle emphasises that the uncanny 'has to do with a sense of ourselves as double, split, at odds with ourselves' (2003, 12). The dragon is uncanny because of its strange familiarity, which makes it more eerily frightening than it was in its previous monstrous state.

[33] According to Royle (2003, 1), the uncanny 'can take the form of something familiar unexpectedly arising in a strange and unfamiliar context'.

The past must thus be abhorrent: an awareness of the past brings with it an awareness of the passing of the present and signifies an end which, to men, is both abhorrent and monstrous and, at the same time, the biggest fact of life. There is no shortage of monstrous father-figures in myths that are constructed to deal with this paradox: that the givers of life may also signify the end of life (see for example Warner 1998, 48–77). One need only mention the myth of Saturn, well-known to medieval Icelanders and expressed in various ways in their writing (Ármann Jakobsson 2005, 312–15).

Although the giants of the Eddas provide perhaps the most common expression of the ancestor as an ogre (Ármann Jakobsson 2008), the monstrosity of death is also perfectly symbolised in a huge and monstrous being such as a dragon, and the conflicting relationship of fatherhood, encompassing both past and future, is clearly present in the dragon-slaying of Sigurðr. Killing the dragon signifies the birth of the hero but at the same time the death of the dragon also signifies the hero's end, as the dragon thus necessarily becomes a paternal figure to the hero. If the hero is erotic in his energetic youth, the dragon is thanatic as he symbolises the mortal parent.

This dialogue about fatherhood is not preserved in any existing narratives about Ragnarr but the legend is clearly the same: Ragnarr is a youth since only a youth can kill the dragon, and indeed Ragnarr is later killed by serpents of far lesser stature: the adders of the wormpit where he is thrown by King Ælla (158). Killing a dragon is no feat for a mature ruler; only youths can be fearless enough. Thus the dragon becomes an important emblem of teenage power in the Middle Ages, signifying that key characteristic of youth which is physical fortitude. Although, as is also shown in *Vǫlsunga saga*, the youth may not cope so well with the rest of his life after he has killed the dragon.

Bibliography

Aarne, Antti and Stith Thompson 1961. *The Types of the Folktale: A Classification and Bibliography.*
Andersson, Theodore M. 1980. *The Legend of Brynhild.* Islandica 43.
Andersson, Theodore M. 1999. 'Goðafræði eða sagnfræði?: Dæmi Völsunga sögu'. In *Heiðin minni: Greinar um fornar bókmenntir.* Ed. Haraldur Bessason and Baldur Hafstað, 91–101.
Ármann Jakobsson 1997. *Í leit að konungi: Konungsmynd íslenskra konungasagna.*
Ármann Jakobsson 1998. 'History of the Trolls? *Bárðar saga* as an Historical Narrative'. *Saga-Book* XXV, 53–71.
Ármann Jakobsson 2003. 'Snorri and His Death: Youth, Violence, and Autobiography in Medieval Iceland'. *Scandinavian Studies* 75, 317–40.
Ármann Jakobsson 2005. 'The Specter of Old Age: Nasty Old Men in the Sagas of Icelanders'. *Journal of English and Germanic Philology* 104, 297–325.

Ármann Jakobsson 2008. 'A Contest of Cosmic Fathers: God and Giant in Vafþrúðnismál'. *Neophilologus* 92, 263–77.
Ármann Jakobsson 2009. 'The Fearless Vampire Killers: A Note about the Icelandic *Draugr* and Demonic Contamination in *Grettis saga*'. *Folklore* 120.
Ármann Jakobsson 2010. 'Íslenskir draugar frá landnámi til lúterstrúar: Inngangur að draugafræðum'. *Skírnir* 184, 187–210.
Ásdís Egilsdóttir 1999. 'Drekar, slöngur og heilög Margrét'. In *Heiðin minni: Greinar um fornar bókmenntir*. Ed. Haraldur Bessason and Baldur Hafstað, 241–56.
Bascom, William 1965. 'The Forms of Folklore: Prose Narratives'. *Journal of American Folklore* 78, 3–20.
Beowulf and the Fight at Finnsburg 1950. Ed. Fr. Klaeber. 3rd edition.
Bjarnar saga Hítdœlakappa. In *Borgfirðinga saga* 1938. Ed. Sigurður Nordal and Guðni Jónsson. Íslenzk fornrit III.
Brennu-Njáls saga 1954. Ed. Einar Ólafur Sveinsson. Íslenzk fornrit XII.
Burrow, J. A. 1986. *The Ages of Man: A Study in Medieval Writing and Thought*.
Carroll, Noel 2010. "The Fear of Fear Itself: The Philosophy of Halloween". In 'Zombies, Vampires, and Philosophy: New Life for the Undead'. Ed. Richard Green and K. Silem Mohammad. *Popular Culture and Philosophy* 49, 223–35.
Cikalmini, M. 1966. 'Grettir and Ketill Hængr, the Giant-Killers'. *Arv* 22, 136–55.
Ciklamini, M. 1971. 'The Problem of Starkaðr'. *Scandinavian Studies* 43, 169–88.
Clover, Carol 1993. 'Regardless of Sex: Men, Women, and Power in Early Northern Europe'. *Speculum* 68, 363–87.
Cohen, Jeffrey Jerome 1996. 'Monster Culture (Seven Theses)'. *Monster Theory: Reading Culture*, 3–25.
Csapo, Eric 2005. *Theories of Mythology*.
Dinzelbacher, Peter 1996. *Angst im Mittelalter: Teufels-, Todes- und Gotteserfahrung, Mentalitätsgeschichte und Ikonographie*.
Duby, Georges 1968. 'In Northwestern France: The "Youth" in Twelfth-Century Aristocratic Society'. In *Lordship and Community in Medieval Europe: Selected Readings*. Ed. Fredric L. Cheyette. New York, 198–209.
Eliade, Mircea 1974 [1954]. *The Myth of the Eternal Return or, Cosmos and History*. Trans. Willard R. Trask.
Evans, Jonathan 2005. 'As Rare As They are Dire: Old Norse Dragons, Beowulf, and the Deutsche Mythologie'. In *The Shadow-Walkers: Jacob Grimm's Mythology of the Monstrous*. Ed. Tom Shippey, 207–69.
Flateyjarbók = *Flateyjarbok: En Samling af norske Konge-Sagaer med indskudte mindre Fortællinger om Begivenheder i og undenfor Norge samt Annaler*. 1860–68. Ed. Guðbrandur Vigfússon and C. R. Unger.
Freud, Sigmund 1973 [1955]. *The Complete Psychological Works* XVII. Ed. James Strachey, Anna Freud, Alix Strachey and Alan Tyson.
Freud, Sigmund 1973 [1955]. *The Complete Psychological Works* XVIII. Ed. James Strachey, Anna Freud, Alix Strachey and Alan Tyson.
Hastrup, Kirsten 1987. 'Presenting the Past: Reflections on Myth and History'. *Folk* 29, 257–69.

'Interrogating genre in the fornaldarsögur: Round-table discussion' 2006. *Viking and Medieval Scandinavia* 2, 275–96.

Jón Friðjónsson 1993. *Mergur málsins: íslensk orðatiltæki, uppruni, saga og notkun*.

Lindow, John 1978. 'Hreiðars þáttr heimska and AT 326: An Old Icelandic Novella and an International Folktale'. *Arv* 34, 152–79.

Lönnroth, Lars 1976. *Njáls Saga: A Critical Introduction*.

Marcuse, Herbert 1972. *Eros and Civilization: A Philosophical Inquiry into Freud with a new preface by the author*.

May, Rollo 1972. *Power and Innocence: A Search for the Sources of Violence*.

McTurk, Rory 1991. *Studies in Ragnars saga loðbrókar and its Major Scandinavian Analogues*.

Morkinskinna 1932. Ed. Finnur Jónsson.

Poetic Edda = Edda: Die Lieder des Codex Regius nebst verwandten Denkmälern 1962. Ed. G. Neckel, rev. H. Kuhn.

Physiologus i to islandske bearbejdelser 1889. Ed. Verner Dahlerup.

Riches, Samantha J. E. 2003. 'Encountering the Monstrous: Saints and Dragons in Medieval Thought'. In *The Monstrous Middle Ages*. Ed. Bettina Bildhauer and Robert Mills, 196–218.

Rowe, Elizabeth Ashman 2005. *The Development of Flateyjarbók: Iceland and the Norwegian Dynastic Crisis of 1389*. The Viking Collection 15.

Rowe, Elizabeth Ashman 2006. 'Qvid Sigvardus cum Christo: Moral Interpretations of Sigurðr Fáfnisbani in Old Norse Literature'. *Viking and Medieval Scandinavia* 2, 167–200.

Royle, Nicholas 2003. *The Uncanny*.

Saxo Grammaticus. *Gesta Danorum: Danmarkshistorien* 2005: 2. Ed. Karsten Friis-Jensen and Peter Zeeberg.

Sävborg, Daniel 2009. 'Avstånd, gräns och förundran: Möten med de övernaturliga i islänningasagan'. In *Greppaminni: Rit til heiðurs Vésteini Ólasyni sjötugum*. Ed. Margrét Eggertsdóttir et al., 323–49.

Schjødt, Jens Peter 1994. 'Heltedigtning og initiationsritualer: En religionsfænomenologisk analyse af den "unge" Sigurd Fafnersbanes historie'. In *Myte og ritual i det førkristne Norden: Et symposium*, 113–27.

Schjødt, Jens Peter 2008. *Initiation between two Worlds: Structure and Symbolism in Pre-Christian Scandinavian Mythology*. The Viking Collection 17.

Slencska, Notger 2007. 'Der endgültige Schrecken: Das Jüngste Gericht und die Angst in der Religion des Mittelalters'. *Das Mittelalter* 12, 97–112.

Sverrir Jakobsson 2005. *Við og veröldin: Heimsmynd Íslendinga 1100–1400*.

Tolkien, J. R. R. 1936. '*Beowulf*: The Monsters and the Critics'. *Proceedings of the British Academy*, 245–95. [repr. 1977].

Vǫlsunga saga ok Ragnars saga loðbrókar 1908. Ed. Magnus Olsen. Samfund til udgivelse af gammel nordisk litteratur 36.

Warner, Marina 1998. *No Go The Bogeyman: Scaring, Lulling, and Making Mock*.

Watkins, Calvert 1995. *How to Kill a Dragon: Aspects of Indo-European Poetics*.

Þorskfirðinga saga. In *Harðar saga* 1991. Ed. Þórhallur Vilmundarson and Bjarni Vilhjálmsson. Íslenzk fornrit XIII.

ÞÓRA AND ÁSLAUG IN *RAGNARS SAGA LOÐBRÓKAR*. WOMEN, DRAGONS AND DESTINY

CAROLYNE LARRINGTON

Introduction

Ragnarr loðbrók is one of a very few Germanic heroes to fight a real poison-spewing dragon; he, Beowulf and Bǫðvarr Bjarki belong to a select group, along with Ragnarr's future, if posthumous, father-in-law, Sigurðr Fáfnisbani. Ragnarr's fellow *fornaldarsaga* heroes in fact have surprisingly little to do with dragons of the impeccably serpentine kind. *Hrólfs saga kraka* is the only other saga which seems to have an authentically Germanic dragon, one which flies like the *Beowulf* dragon, and whose blood and heart transform the man who consumes them, just as Fáfnir's does. Ketill hængr kills a monster which has coils and a tail like a serpent, though it is winged like a dragon, with fire coming from its eyes and mouth (*Ketils saga hængs* 1942, 246–47). Ketill's feat is an adolescent rite of passage, which earns him his father's approval and the nickname *hængr*, after he modestly claims that the animal he killed was an unusual kind of salmon (Larrington 2008). Yngvarr víðfǫrli meets some exotic, un-Germanic dragons, including the *Über*-dragon Jakulus during his eastern voyages (*Yngvars saga víðfǫrla* 1910). The other dragons of the *fornaldarsaga* corpus seem either to be avatars of trolls, giants or magical humans (*Gǫngu-Hrólfs saga*, *Hálfdanar saga Eysteinssonar*), or foreboding dream-figures (*Sǫgubrot*, *Hrómundar saga Gripssonar*).

Ragnarr's serpent belongs to a different category from the other *fornaldarsaga* dragons; it does not fly, it is not fiery, nor is it a transformed human nor a psychic symbol of trouble to come. It is essentially an overgrown snake, resembling the pairs of terrifying serpents encountered more than once in Saxo's *Gesta Danorum*, from which it probably derives. The fight between hero and serpent shares details with the European folk-tale tradition about dragons and their vanquishers: the dragon's voraciousness makes it impossible to tolerate, the hero must devise special ingenious armour to overcome it, the fight also functions as a rite of passage for the young hero. The dragon and the dragon-fight(er) have been frequently investigated in Germanic, and indeed Indo-European heroic literatures (Watkins 1995; Lionarons 1998). In this essay, however, I shall investigate the rather less fully researched links between the female characters—in particular the heroine—of the saga and the dragons, past and present, which shape their fates. The serpent (*ormr*) which Ragnarr kills is monstrous in all versions of the story, and may be regarded as a dragon, for it is morphologically identical to Fáfnir, lacking wings and spitting poison. Sigurðr clearly identifies Fáfnir at first sight as a *dreki*, noting that he is considerably larger than the *lyngormr* which Reginn had misleadingly claimed to be his brother's new form (*Vǫlsunga saga* 1906–08, 33, 41).

Ragnars saga loðbrókar is preserved in NKS 1824b 4to, dating from around 1400, where it is coupled with *Vǫlsunga saga*, and also in a poorly-preserved and fragmentary state in AM 147 4to, containing a version from a slightly different tradition. The constituent elements of the narratives about Ragnarr and his second wife Áslaug are widespread in Scandinavian tradition; the relationship between the different preserved versions of the stories is a complex one, laid bare by Rory McTurk (McTurk 1991). This essay mainly discusses the version of the saga in 1824b, but it will also draw upon other analogues and possible sources. The saga begins with the childhood misfortunes of Áslaug, daughter of Sigurðr the dragon-slayer, a character introduced briefly as an infant in *Vǫlsunga saga* (1906–10, 69). Only a small, extremely faded and hard-to-read title: *Sagha Raghnars lodbrokar*, of roughly the same size as the chapter headings within the sagas, indicates that the new saga has begun on fol. 51r, but the first chapter of *Ragnars saga* assumes that its audience remembers both Áslaug and her foster-father Heimir from fol. 32v earlier in the manuscript. Next in the saga comes the exciting battle of Ragnarr against the monster-serpent which protects the bower of Þóra, daughter of the jarl of Gautland, whom Ragnarr later marries. Subsequently Áslaug, Ragnarr's second wife, is about to be put aside in favour of the daughter of King Eysteinn of Sweden when she reveals her dragon-slaying lineage, and, as proof, bears a son, Sigurðr ormr-í-auga, who carries the sign of his grandfather's feat in his eyes. Finally Ragnarr disregards his wife's wise advice not to invade England with too few ships, and despite his possession of a shirt of invulnerability given to him by his queen, perishes in a snake-pit. King Ella of Northumbria is clever enough to recognise the shirt's function and strip it from his victim. According to AM 147 4to Ragnarr dies reciting the *Krákumál*, a heroic death-song which was much admired and much translated in the eighteenth-century revival of interest in Norse heroic poetry; the poem follows the saga in 1824b (Shippey 1998; Clunies Ross 2001, 90–131; McTurk 2007a). *Ragnars saga* thus features two women with serpent or dragon connections: Þóra, Ragnarr's first wife and Áslaug, his second.

Ragnarr and Áslaug

The ruler of Gautland, a certain Herrauðr, delights in sending a gift every morning to his beautiful daughter Þóra borgarhjǫrtr. One day he sends to her bower a pretty little *lyngormr*, for the moment a much smaller version of the same kind of creature as Fáfnir is. Þóra keeps the serpent in a box and nourishes it by putting a gold piece under it every day. The snake grows, as does the gold pile, and eventually it outgrows the box, and indeed Þóra's bower. By now it is becoming a nuisance; it lies wrapped round the bower with its head meeting its tail (much like the Miðgarðsormr) and it has become *illr . . . viðreignar* 'nasty to deal with' (*Ragnars saga*, 117).[1] It maintains friendly relations with Þóra and the man who brings it an ox every day as food; the main problem with the beast is that it has grown too big and consumes too many economic resources. Its behaviour is similar to the dragons of folk-tale, who do not directly threaten the settlements near which they live, and are often tolerated until the number of cattle they consume becomes a nuisance (Briggs 1970–71, BI 159–72). These dragons differ from Beowulf's dragon, which launches an immediate attack on the king's mead-hall and the settlement of the Geats when enraged by theft from its treasure; such aggressive and fiery, flying dragons demand immediate action. Þóra's father decrees that the gold and the girl will be given to whoever can kill the serpent, and Ragnarr, son of King Sigurðr hringr of Denmark, dares the feat. He prepares a shaggy cape and breeches, and has them covered in pitch. He makes his way to Gautland, rolls in sand which adheres to the pitch, and then, having loosened the nail securing the head of his spear, kills the dragon by stabbing it in the back. The serpent vomits a great wave of presumably poisonous blood which strikes Ragnarr, but does not harm him because of his protective clothing, and the hero makes off, leaving the spear-head in the dragon's corpse and reciting a verse which Þóra hears and understands. Ragnarr later lays claim to the serpent-slaying feat and proves his identity by showing the shaft which fits the spear; this motif suggests the introduction of a false claimant to the reward, as in the later Faeroese ballad sequence *Ragnarskvæði* and as in the story of Tristan (McTurk 1991, 58–59, 235–39; Mundt 1971, 131–33, 139–40), but no false claimant appears in the 1824b version. Ragnarr marries Þóra and becomes famous across the North for his feat. To Ragnarr's great distress, Þóra dies in giving birth to her second son; he abandons his rule and returns to Viking activities.

[1] All references to *Ragnars saga* are to Olsen's edition (1906–08). The spelling has been normalised for the sake of clarity.

Later, Ragnarr's men catch sight of Kráka, the foster-daughter of cruel and avaricious peasants living in southern Norway. Kráka is really Áslaug Sigurðardóttir (or Brynhildardóttir), brought there by her foster-father Heimir, who was murdered by the peasants for his treasure. Despite the peasant-woman's attempts to hide her beauty, Kráka-Áslaug is astonishingly lovely, as Ragnarr's men report to him. Ragnarr summons her to his ship; in an attempt to discover whether she is as clever as she is beautiful, he sets conditions as to how she must come to him: *'hvarki vil ek, at hon sé klædd né óklædd, hvarki mett né ómett, ok fari hon þó eigi ein saman, ok skal henni þó engi maðr fylgja'* "I want her to be neither clothed nor unclothed, neither fed nor unfed, and she may not come by herself nor shall anyone come with her" (*Ragnars saga* 124). Kráka fulfils his demand by going to Ragnarr's ship wearing a fishing-net and covered by her hair which extends down to her ankles. She is accompanied by her faithful dog, and has licked a leek whose smell is apparent on her breath. Ragnarr's men kill her dog after it bites the hand Ragnarr extends in greeting, despite the promises of safe-conduct made to her: *er eigi betr griðum haldit við hana enn svá* 'the truce with her was maintained no better than this', comments the author (*Ragnars saga*, 125). The slaying of the dog suggests a degree of impetuosity on the part of Ragnarr's men, a quality shared by their lord. Ragnarr desires Kráka and offers her a silk shirt which had been Þóra's. Kráka refuses it, saying that she is not worthy of such finery, but she agrees to marry him on his return from his voyage. Ragnarr waits until Kráka has come with him to Denmark and marries her legally. However, when she asks for three days' grace before consummating the union, warning that their first child will be born deformed, he takes her against her will, and their first son is Ívarr inn beinlauss 'the Boneless'.

Kráka gives birth to three more sons, then Ragnarr is persuaded by his men to agree to marry the daughter of King Eysteinn of Sweden in preference to his apparently low-status wife. Although Ragnarr's retinue is pledged to secrecy, Kráka learns of the plan to repudiate her from some birds, whose language she understands—a trait presumably inherited from her father—and declares her true parentage and origins to Ragnarr. When he does not believe her, she pledges that the son she is expecting will be born with a serpent in his eye, as indeed turns out to be the case. Ragnarr acknowledges this in a series of verses, discussed below.

After Ragnarr calls off his marriage to Eysteinn's daughter, the two sons of Þóra seize the opportunity to go raiding in Sweden and are captured and killed. Verses asking Áslaug to avenge them are reported to her and she rallies her reluctant sons, aided by the *bráðgǫrr* 'precocious' three-year-old Sigurðr who urges his brothers, to undertake a revenge expedition (see Larrington 2009a for discussion of this episode). Áslaug leads a land army to Sweden while her sons go by ship; as a consequence of this expedition she changes her name for the third and last time to Randalín. This name turns up around 1230 in Iceland as a female name among the Oddverjar, suggesting that this version of the story was already known by then in Iceland (McTurk 1991, 179).

Ragnarr's sons subdue much of northwestern Europe, to the extent that Ragnarr feels his reputation is diminishing, and he sets off to England against Randalín's advice (Rowe 2008; Rowe forthcoming). Showing the kind of prudential qualities we would expect from the daughter of the wisdom-dispensing valkyrie—for Sigrdrífa's Eddic wisdom is ascribed to Brynhildr in *Vǫlsunga saga*—Randalín deploys the good sense which is also typical of *fornaldarsaga* queens (see Jóhanna Friðriksdóttir, this volume). Randalín also gives Ragnarr the shirt of invulnerability, paralleling the special clothing Ragnarr had prepared for the dragon-fight and forming a counter-gift to Þóra's silk shirt which Ragnarr had offered to her on first meeting (McTurk 1991, 74). Later analogues such as *Ragnarskvæði* suggest that the shirt would have fitted only Ragnarr's destined second wife as prophesied by the dying Þóra, a frequently-encountered folk-tale motif (McTurk 1991, 80, 178–79). That is almost the last we hear of Randalín in the saga; she eventually becomes an old woman and her final verse laments the death of her son Hvítserkr (*Ragnars saga*, 168–69). In *Þáttr af Ragnarssonum* (a text found in *Hauksbók*) Randalín has a more extended career: she raises the children of Sigurðr ormr-í-auga with the help of a certain Helgi hvassi after her youngest son dies in battle; here she speaks another verse in lament for him which is not evidenced elsewhere in surviving tradition.

Áslaug, then, forms a crucial link between the central European lineage of Sigurðr's family and the lineage of both the kings of Denmark and the kings of Norway through male and female lines. As Torfi Tulinius (2003, 82) has noted, Áslaug's existence makes it possible to continue the Volsungs' lineage after the death of Sigurðr and his son Sigmundr, by grafting it onto the Skjǫldungr line in Denmark, through the marital relationship with Ragnar loðbrók. The comparative success and failure of the dynasties of Sigurðr's two daughters Áslaug and Svanhildr, juxtaposed in NKS 1824b 4to—and the larger relationships between *Vǫlsunga saga* and *Ragnars saga* in that manuscript—are discussed in Larrington 2009a and 2009b.

Ragnarr, Þóra and the Dragon

Scholarly investigation of the fight between Ragnarr and the dragon has been rather limited. It is normally understood in the context of the mythological tale-type of the hero versus the dragon, familiar enough in Indo-European myth (see Watkins 1995; Lionarons 1998, 50–51; Evans 2005). The dragon-fight is only one of Ragnarr's adventures in the earliest full version of his career found in Saxo Grammaticus's *Gesta Danorum*, Book IX (Ellis Davidson and Fisher 1998, 281–91); Saxo's version offers some interesting points of comparison and contrast with the saga. Here Regnerus (Ragnarr) overcomes a pair of serpents whom the princess nourishes with a carcass of beef a day rather than with a gold-hoard, and thus he wins Thora as his second wife. Regnerus has a succession of wives and many sons by them, before he dies of snakebites in Ella's prison. One of Regnerus's sons is named Siwardus *serpentini oculi*, and, according to Saxo, he acquires his snake mark when an Odinic figure, Roftar (= ON *Hroptr*, an Óðinn-name) comes to minister to him when he is injured after a battle. Although the mark may commemorate his father's feat, Saxo does not make this suggestion, noting that the serpent primarily signals Siwardus's own ferocity and the pact he makes to dedicate his battle victims to Odin (Ellis Davidson and Fisher 1998, 281–83). The snake mark has no obvious association with Siwardus's mother, Thora. Nor does Áslaug appear in Saxo, though Regnerus's third wife Svanloga has some features in common with her. Svanloga has a valkyrie-type name while Áslaug has a valkyrie mother; both women bear several sons to Regnerus and both urge revenge for a dead son or stepsons on reluctant male kindred. Áslaug urges her sons to avenge their stepbrothers in the saga, Svanloga admonishes Regnerus not to give way to grief for Vithsercus in Saxo (Ellis Davidson and Fisher 1998, 289).

Þóra and her serpent coexist cheerfully in *Ragnars saga*; although the serpent presents a drain on the land's economic resources, he does not physically threaten Þóra. Rather the dragon represents a functional obstacle to the marriage of the now-nubile young woman; she cannot wed until her dowry and her person are liberated from the serpent. The dragon operates to protect Þóra's chastity: this function is made explicit in an earlier serpent-tale in the *Gesta Danorum*, in Book VII (Ellis Davidson and Fisher 1998, 210–12). In this narrative, a young woman, Alvild, rears a pair of serpents, explicitly given to her by her father in order to protect her chastity. When the warrior Alf kills them as a condition of becoming her suitor, the girl is ready to marry him. However Alvild's mother rebukes her for being immodestly eager to give herself to the first dragon-killer to come along and, chastened, she runs off to sea to become a pirate. Alf eventually tracks Alvild and her female shipmates down, and he and his men overcome them in battle, conquering the women 'not with weapons, but with kisses' (Ellis Davidson and Fisher 1998, 212). The dragons long forgotten, Alvild gives up piracy, dons women's clothing and goes back to weaving and, ultimately, wifehood; conventional if unexciting female destinies, especially in comparison with Áslaug's post-marital career.

In this narrative, as, I suggest, at a submerged level in *Ragnars saga*, the dragon(s) represents a very clear impediment to the marriage of a young woman. At first the creatures are effective guardians, co-operating in the father's plan to keep his daughter chaste, but when he gauges his daughter to be ready for marriage, the obstacles and her resistance must be eliminated. Þóra seems also to regard the dragon as an ally up to the point when Ragnarr appears; her coexistence with the serpent invites the monster's interpretation in courtly terms, as an embodiment of feminine *danger*—the resistance which the decent woman shows to the male wooer (as personified in the thirteenth-century French dream vision *Le Roman de la Rose*). Indeed, the dragon could well have been understood as performing this function in the context of the 1400 date of NKS 1824b 4to; by then such courtly tropes were well known in Iceland.

Þóra is the sole witness to Ragnarr's feat in vanquishing the dragon. Its death not only removes the physical obstacle to marriage—for the serpent was literally sitting on her dowry—but any psychological resistance on Þóra's part seems to disappear too. Þóra is distinctly interested in the dragon-slayer; she asks Ragnarr his name '*eða hvern hann vili nú finna*' "and whom he might be looking for" (*Ragnars saga*, 118), a flirtatious question which draws the hero's attention away from the defeated dragon towards herself. Ragnarr replies with the saga's first verse: while he does not vouchsafe his identity, he addresses her as '*litfǫgr kona*' "beautiful lady" and boasts that he is only fifteen years old as he performs this prodigious deed. Þóra's enquiry suggests that she expects that the dragon-slayer will become her husband. Unlike Alvild, who 'warmly praised her wooer's excellence' before her mother castigated her for 'gazing with an unprincipled mind' and being 'tickled by [Alf's] enticing appearance', (Ellis Davidson and Fisher 1998, 211), Þóra is troubled by her wooer's looks which—partly thanks to his costume—are not prepossessing. Indeed she wonders *hvárt hann er mennskr maðr eða eigi, fyrir því at henni þykkir vǫxtr hans vera svá mikill sem sagt er frá óvættum á þeim aldri sem hann hafði* 'whether he is human or not, since his size seems to her as great as that of monsters is said to be, considering his age' (*Ragnars saga*, 119). Þóra retires to her chamber and goes back to sleep. Her doubts must have resolved themselves, for later she advises her father to call an assembly so that the dragon-slayer may make himself known, deliberately setting in motion the process by which the unknown dragon-slayer becomes first her socially acknowledged suitor and then her husband. Þóra's oscillation between attraction and repulsion, though adequately motivated by Ragnarr's unusual appearance, emphasises that she too is undergoing a rite of passage, just as much as the hero of the dragon-fight, making the transition from the protected, self-sufficient condition of girlhood to the desiring socially mature state of female adulthood (see McTurk 2007b for a discussion of Áslaug and initation ritual).

Áslaug and Mélusine

The serpent symbolism activated in the context of Áslaug's role in the saga is quite different from the dragon's role as guardian of Þóra's chastity and symbol of *danger*, which, though underdeveloped, seems to be present in the early part of the narrative. The genetic marker of the serpent in the eye, which may originally have signalled Ragnarr's heroic deed (though, as we have seen, Saxo does not make that connection), is transferred to Áslaug both in *Ragnars saga* and in later ballad tradition. In the Faroese ballad *Ragnarskvæði*, Áslaug herself has a snake mark on or near her eye, unremarked on in some variants, but very obvious in others (McTurk 1991, 80); in *Ragnars saga* no serpent sign is visible on her. Yet, since Áslaug is always already the daughter of Sigurðr from the moment her story emerges, as McTurk argues (1991, 156), it is not surprising that she too should bear, internally if not externally, the sign of her dragon-slayer father. The potency of this serpentine connection in Áslaug's genes, although adequately motivated by the question of lineage, recalls another powerful serpent-woman: the French ancestress figure, Mélusine (Jean d'Arras 1974; Coudrette 1982; Harf-Lancner 1984). The fairy Mélusine takes in hand the rather luckless nobleman Raimondin. Insisting that he marry her according to the rites of the Catholic church, she brings about a change in her husband's fortune and status, helping him to obtain land by means of the same folklore trick by which Ívarr inn beinlauss gains the territory on which to found London (AT K 185 'Deceptive Land Purchase'; Jean d'Arras 1974, 31, 33–35; Coudrette 1982, 131–32, 136–39; *Ragnars saga*, 164–65). Imposing a taboo on Raimondin, that he should never seek to discover what she does on Saturdays, Mélusine shows herself to be both an effective and a fecund *grande dame*: founder of cities, builder of churches and mother of many sons (for Mélusine's achievements as foundress figure, see Le Goff and Ladurie 1971). When Raimondin privately breaks the Saturday taboo and discovers her secret, glimpsing her in the bath and seeing that she has a serpent's tail (Jean d'Arras 1974, 241–42; Coudrette 1982, 210–12), the relationship nevertheless continues, for Mélusine is ignorant of Raimondin's betrayal. It is only when, in the course of an argument about the behaviour of one of their sons, Raimondin publicly accuses her of being a snake that the marriage breaks down (Jean d'Arras 1974, 255–56; Coudrette 1982, 237). Mélusine must leave her family forever, and revert to half-serpentine form; her hopes of gaining an immortal soul and salvation are destroyed by her husband's indiscretion.

Like Áslaug's eldest and youngest sons, Ívarr inn beinlauss and Sigurðr ormr-í-auga, most of Mélusine's sons are physically unusual, including the eldest. Notably, a number of them have strange eyes, whether malformed, miscoloured, too few or too many. Geoffrey la grand dent, the most heroic of her sons, has normal eyes, but his distinguishing feature is a great tooth which protrudes through his cheek. The tooth does not inhibit Geoffrey's courage and ferocity, for he becomes the ancestor of the well-known noble house of Lusignan in Poitou. Raimondin had encountered Mélusine for the first time in a moment of crisis; out hunting he has thrown his spear at a boar and has missed, killing his lord and patron in error. Mélusine suggests a strategy for covering up the exact circumstances of the Count's death; Raimondin is to declare that the Count's horse bolted and that he does not know what happened to him. When the bodies of the Count and the boar (whom Raimondin had eventually succeeded in killing) are found, the young man escapes suspicion and censure. Geoffrey's boar-like tusk thus writes on the son's body the hidden truth in his father's history, just as Sigurðr ormr-í-auga embodies the presence of dragon-killing in the lineage. Lionarons (1998, 50) suggests that Ívarr's disability may also reflect serpentine qualities, though the fact that Áslaug tries to postpone the consummation in order to prevent the birth of a boneless son (explicitly mentioned in st. 6, and thus probably also present in AM 147 4to) implies that she does not view her eldest son's debilitating condition as positively as her youngest son's distinguishing mark.

I do not intend to argue either that the tale of Mélusine has influenced the Áslaug story, for the recorded French versions of the tale were composed in the late fourteenth century, nor that Áslaug's story could have filtered south to France and influenced the development of the Mélusine legend. Rather, the common features of the serpent-woman story point to the influence on both legend complexes of a shared archetype (see Alban 2003 for the mythological history of serpent-women). The snake-women Áslaug and Mélusine mother broods of strange but heroic sons, exhibiting prophetic powers and wise leadership in contrast to relatively ineffectual husbands.

Both women communicate and endure the breaking of a powerful taboo, but nevertheless achieve culturally highly valued feats: land clearance and city building in the case of Mélusine; exhorting and participating in revenge for her predecessor's children and weaving a shirt of invulnerability, providing the kind of protection associated with valkyries, in the case of Áslaug. Comparison with Mélusine illuminates how multivalent Áslaug's serpentine connections are; not only does she facilitate the reproduction of patrilineal genetic markers, her serpent-inheritance shapes both her destiny as wife to Ragnarr and her understanding and social practice of maternality (Larrington 2009a).

Dragons in the next generation

Whose are the dragon genes which Áslaug transmits? Ragnarr's feat as dragon-slayer is an initiatory adventure, the first one the hero undertakes, and, as Ármann Jakobsson (this volume) points out, it is the only notable feat ascribed to him in a saga in which he is far surpassed by his sons. Ragnarr's relative ineffectuality contrasts powerfully with the spectacular achievements of Saxo's Regnerus, who defeats Charlemagne and conquers territories from Britain to the eastern Baltic, holding sway over most of Scandinavia, even if his rule is frequently disrupted by revolts among the mutinous northern tribes. These empire-building feats are transferred to his sons in the saga tradition (Rowe 2008; Rowe forthcoming). Sigurðr too undertakes an initiatory adventure of sorts in killing Fáfnir, though he postpones the attack until he has fulfilled the primary social requirement of avenging his father. Dragon-slaying seems then to inscribe itself in the killer's DNA, but the provenance of the serpentine mark has become unclear by the time it manifests itself in the eye of Ragnarr's fifth and last son by Áslaug. The three-stanza sequence which forms the narrative core of the episode is found in full only in 1824b 4to, but fragments of it are readable in AM 147 4to. In this sequence Ragnarr heralds his son's ancestry, emphasising in the first two stanzas the child's maternal line:

Sigurðr mun sveinn of heitinn,	Sigurðr the boy will be called;
sá mun orrostur heyja,	he will wage battles;
mjǫk líkr vera móður	he will be very like his mother
ok mǫgr fǫður kallaðr;	and called the son of his father;
sá mun Óðins ættar	he will in Óðinn's line
yfir*bátr* vera heitinn, *þátt 147	be called the most prominent one,
þeim er ormr í auga,	there is a serpent in his eye,
er annan lét svelta.	which made another die (?)

(*Ragnars saga* 136, st. 8)

Ragnarr notes the child's descent; the verse draws a distinction which may be meaningful between the child's physical resemblance to his mother and his legal recognition by his father (*kallaðr mǫgr fǫður*). Olsen construes *móður fǫður* as two genitives ('called a boy very like his mother's father') (*Ragnars saga*, 200), excising Ragnarr's paternal contribution altogether in favour of Áslaug's own father. The baby is also said to be descended from Óðinn's lineage (via grandfather Sigurðr's Volsung bloodline); twice as much weight is placed on the maternal as the paternal line. The sign of the snake in his eye indicates the serpent, *er annan lét svelta* 'which made another die'. This line is obscure: the subject of the clause ought logically to be *annarr* (nom.), so that the reference would be to the earlier slayings of serpents by Sigurðr's father and / or grandfather. *Annan* (acc.) is clear enough in the manuscript, however (fol. 62v). Olsen emends the problem away, substituting *es ǫrn lætrat svelta* 'who did not let the eagle starve', while Bugge, as Olsen notes, construes *er annan let svelta* with *Óðins ættar yfirbátr* (or *þátt*), taking l. 7 as parenthetical, thus: 'He (who has a serpent in his eye) will be called the most prominent offshoot of Óðinn's descendant, the one who killed another (serpent)'. Bugge thus designates Sigurðr Sigmundarson as having slain serpent number two, while the mark his grandson bears is understood as serpent number one (*Ragnars saga*, 200–01), a suggestion which seems entirely plausible. However l. 8 is construed, and whether or not we accept Olsen's interpretation of the sense of *móður fǫður*, Ragnarr's act of fathering and the understanding of the eye-serpent as a marker of his feat has been subordinated to the superiority of Sigurðr Fáfnisbani's bloodline, and it appears that the baby's eye should be understood as showing the sign of his grandfather's triumph.

The next stanza, in kenning-heavy language, also emphasises the maternal line and the brilliance of the baby's gaze:

Brynhildar lízk brǫgnum	To men seems Brynhildr's
brúnstein hafa fránan	to have a shining brow-stone > EYE
dóttur mǫgr enn dýri	daughter's precious son
ok dyggligast hjarta,	and the bravest of hearts,
sjá berr alla ýta	he will have authority over all men,
undleygs boði magni	the wound-flame's messenger > WARRIOR
Buðla niðr, er baugi,	the precocious descendant of Buðli,
bráðgǫrr, hatar rauðum.	who hates the red-gold ring > GENEROUS MAN.

(*Ragnars saga* 136, st. 9)

Here the reference to young Sigurðr's distinguishing feature is not to a serpent-shaped pupil, or a mark, but to the hero's conventional brilliantly-shining eyes (noted in *Rigsþula* 35 and *Vǫlundarkviða* 17, as well as

Fáfnismál 5). This verse may betray the origins of the snake-mark tradition as a literalisation of the shining-eye motif. The older Sigurðr, *Vǫlsunga saga* tells us, also had exceptionally shining eyes, so that no one dared look into them, and he also took the trouble to inscribe the serpent not only on his shield, but on all his weapons (*Vǫlsunga saga* 1906–10, 55–56). The final verse in the sequence confirms the snake-mark as unique to baby Sigurðr and located in his eye; no further ascription to male or female lineage is ventured:

Svá eru engum sveini,	No boy
nema Sigurði einum,	except Sigurðr alone,
í brúnsteinum brúnir	has laid in his browstones > EYES
barðhjarls taumar lagðir;	the brown (or shining) reins of the steep slope? > SNAKE;
sjá hefr dagrýrir dýja,	this brave diminisher of water's shine > GENEROUS MAN
—dælt er hann af því kenna—	—it is easy to recognise him from this—
hvass í hvarma túni	he has gained in the eyelids' field
hring myrkviðar fengit.	the darkwood's ring > SNAKE.

(*Ragnars saga* 136–37, st. 10)

The transfer of the name and mark across lineages thus emphasises the convergence of dragon-killing destinies. Ragnarr's achievement, and indeed his blood-line, is assimilated to his wife's illustrious genetic inheritance. Although the first stanza about Sigurðr ormr-í-auga is ambiguous enough to leave some doubt as to how Ragnarr, as its speaker, interprets his son's distinctive mark—who the other slayer is, whether there is another dragon—the saga prose, and Áslaug herself, make clear that it is her blood, not his, which transmits it. The ballad tradition confirms this appropriation by giving Áslaug her own dragon mark, evidenced in *Ragnarskvæði* (McTurk 1991, 80). Ragnarr's Danish line—the line of the Skjǫldungar—is thus subordinated to the glorious Volsung inheritance, and significantly it is through women—through Áslaug herself and through Ragnhildr her female descendant—that King Haraldr inn hárfagri traces his descent from this illustrious lineage, connected through Ragnarr to the Skjǫldungr dynasty, but also to Sigurðr, and ultimately to Óðinn himself.

The saga not only plays down the value of Ragnarr's dragon-slaying in comparison to the achievement of Sigurðr Fáfnisbani, it also demonstrates how the erstwhile hero's courage shades into a culpable impetuosity as he matures. He does not value Áslaug as he should, or as he would if he knew her true lineage. He permits his men to kill her dog on first meeting; although he respects her wisdom enough to marry her before undertaking a sexual relationship, he does not heed her prophetic wisdom about the consequences of his sexual impatience, breaking a taboo which brings serious disadvantage to his lineage. He shows himself as suggestible when it comes to acquiring a new wife to cement the alliance with the king of Sweden, then, in an act of outrageous bad faith, tries to conceal his new betrothal from his wife. He scoffs at Áslaug's revelation about her parentage until he is given ocular proof of it, is absent for the revenge mission for the children of his beloved Þóra, and is shown up in this respect by his wife and sons. Finally, he undertakes the expedition to England out of jealousy of the reputation of his and Áslaug's sons. Ignoring his wife's advice, he sets off with only two ships; little wonder then that he meets his end in Ella's snakepit. There is a pleasing symmetry about Ragnarr's final act of courageous endurance, matching his first heroic feat. Whether the snake-pit tends to await the serpent-killer is not clear; the pit itself may, as McTurk and de Vries suggest, have been imported from the fate of Gunnarr in Eddic poetry (McTurk 1991, 89; de Vries 1923, 252). It is striking, however, that in some of the ballads it is the father of Kragelil (= Kráka) who perishes in the snakepit—that is, the figure corresponding to Sigurðr himself. Although this detail in the ballad is probably, as McTurk notes, a direct borrowing from the saga tradition, perhaps the symmetry of the dragon-killer coming to a snake-caused end—as indeed Beowulf does—is an essential part of the archetypal narrative (see Lionarons 1998, 6, following Watkins 1995 on the bi-directionality of the serpent-hero encounter).

Áslaug's serpent-eyed son is precocious; his stanza as a three-year-old (surely not unconnected with Egill Skalla-Grímsson's first poetic effort) is instrumental in persuading his elder brothers that their duty is to support their mother in taking vengeance for their step-brothers (Larrington 2009a). Young Sigurðr is a hero like his brothers, but he kills no dragons; his snake-mark is symbolic only, and in the *Ragnars saga* tradition he is overshadowed by Ívarr inn beinlauss in terms of strategic and political achievement. Sigurðr's main claim to fame lies in his royal descendants: the kings of Norway in both saga and *þáttr*, and also the kings of Denmark in *Þáttr af Ragnarssonum*.

Conclusion

Ragnars saga rewrites the symbolism of the Indo-European mythic dragon, distancing the serpent's overall significance in the saga from that of archetypal foe. It is worth noting that Saxo's Regnerus has already conquered Norway and married Lathgertha before he decides to fight Thora's pair of serpents; *Ragnars saga*'s move away from this pattern, and the *Beowulf* model of the dragon-fight as a culminating achievement, towards an understanding of the fight as initiation adventure has probably been influenced by Sigurðr's contest with Fáfnir. This fight, though not Sigurðr's very first heroic adventure, gives rise to his cognomen *Fáfnisbani*, and his feat is commemorated in one of the few stanzas which *Vǫlsunga saga* cites directly:

Sigurðr vá at ormi,	Sigurðr slew the serpent,
enn þat síðan mun	and that will afterwards
engum fyrnask,	be forgotten by no-one,
meðan ǫld lifir.	while people live.

(*Vǫlsunga saga* 1906–10, 71)

Similarly, Ragnarr's fight and his stoically endured snake-pit death are the most notable things about him in his saga. Rather than inaugurating the kind of empire-building career Regnerus enjoys in Saxo, the serpent contest of *Ragnars saga* opens up interesting questions about female rites of passage: Þóra's transformation from chaste serpent-nurturing virgin to young woman eager to marry the monster-killing hero. McTurk has noted the possibility of a female initiatory paradigm operating in the case of Áslaug and her adventures with her peasant foster-parents and her marriage to Ragnarr (McTurk 2007b). Áslaug is undoubtedly the heroine of *Ragnars saga*: all the key verse sequences and their accompanying narrative tell her story, highlighting her unique status as related to two dragon-slayers and capable of transmitting the sign of that relationship through her body. Áslaug is not a mere conduit for masculine bloodlines, however; like the reflex of the serpent-goddess, the French heroine Mélusine, she is a wise, busy and effective queen, supremely loyal to her husband, children and stepchildren. Bjarni Guðnason (1969, 34) regards Áslaug as the saga's central character: *þar sem Áslaug er, þar er hjarta höfundar* 'where Áslaug is, there is the author's heart', he notes; though the expression is sentimental, perhaps, the critical judgement is correct.

Thus the two dragons, the long-dead Fáfnir and Þóra's *lyngormr*, configure the different destinies of Ragnarr's two wives. The *lyngormr* is an index of Þóra's transformation from maiden to wife; her sons, lacking the snake-mark of their progenitor, die pointlessly heroic deaths in Sweden, bringing Þóra's line to an end. Fáfnir's mark on little Sigurðr finally brings Áslaug the respect and status she deserves, both in the eyes of her husband and her sons, allowing her to avenge her stepsons, and ensuring her veneration as ancestress of two royal houses and the greatest Icelandic families of the fourteenth century when her story is preserved (Rowe 2008; forthcoming).

Bibliography

Alban, Gillian 2003. *Melusine the Serpent Goddess in A. S. Byatt's Possession and in Mythology.*
Bjarni Guðnason 1969. 'Gerðir ok ritþróun Ragnars sögu loðbrókar'. In *Einarsbók: Afmæliskveðja til Einars Ól. Sveinsson*. Ed. nokkrir vinir, 28–37.
Briggs, Katharine 1970–71. *A Dictionary of British Folk-Tales in the English Language.* 2 vols.
Clunies Ross, Margaret 2001. *The Old Norse Poetic Translations of Thomas Percy: A New Edition and Commentary.*
Coudrette 1982. *Le Roman de Mélusine ou Histoire de Lusignan.* Ed. E. Roach.
Ellis Davidson, Hilda, ed., and Peter Fisher, trans., 1979–80. *Saxo Grammaticus. The History of the Danes, Books I–IX.*
Evans, Jonathan 2005. '"As Rare As They Are Dire": Old Norse Dragons, *Beowulf* and the *Deutsche Mythologie*'. In *The Shadow-Walkers: Jacob Grimm's Mythology of the Monstrous*. Ed. T. A. Shippey, 207–69.
Gottzmann, Carola 1979. 'Völsunga saga: Legendary history and textual analysis'. In *Preprints of the 4th International Saga Conference*, vol. I.
Harf-Lancner, Laurence 1984. *Les fées au Moyen Age. Morgane et Mélusine ou la naissance des fées.*
Jean d'Arras 1974. *Mélusine: roman du XIVe Siècle.* Ed. L. Stouff.
Ketils saga hængs. In *Fornaldarsögur Norðurlanda* 1942. Ed. Guðni Jónsson and Bjarni Vilhjálmsson. 2 vols.
Larrington, Carolyne 2008. 'Awkward Adolescents: Male Maturation in Norse Literature'. In *Youth and Age in the Medieval North*. Ed. Shannon Lewis-Simpson, 145–60.
Larrington, Carolyne 2009a. 'Stjúpmœðrasögur and Sigurðr's Daughters'. In *Preprint Papers of the Fourteenth International Saga Conference, Uppsala, 9th–14th August 2009*. Ed. A. Ney, H. Williams et al., 568–75.
Larrington, Carolyne 2009b. '*Völsunga saga* and *Ragnars saga*: revisiting the relationship'. Paper given at 'Fornaldarsögur Norðurlanda: Uppruni og þróun'. Ráðstefna í Reykjavík 29. og 30. ágúst 2009.
Le Goff, Jacques and Emmanuel Le Roy Ladurie 1971. 'Mélusine maternelle et défricheuse'. *Annales Economies Sociétés Civilisations* 26, 587–622.
Lionarons, Joyce Tally 1998. *The Medieval Dragon: The Nature of the Beast in Germanic Literature.*
McTurk, Rory 1991. *Studies in Ragnars saga loðbrókar and its major Scandinavian Analogues.*
McTurk, Rory 2007a. 'Samuel Ferguson's "Death-Song" (1833): An Anglo-Irish Response to *Krákumál*'. In *Constructing Nations, Reconstructing Myth: Essays in Honour of T. A. Shippey*. Ed. A. Wawn, with Graham Johnson and John Walter, 167–91.
McTurk, Rory 2007b. 'Male or Female Initiation? The Strange Case of *Ragnars saga*'. In *Reflections on Old Norse Myths*. Ed. Pernille Hermann, Jens Peter Schjødt and Rasmus Tranum Kristensen, 53–73.
Mundt, Marina 1971. 'Omkring dragekampen i Ragnars saga loðbrókar'. *Arv* 27, 121–40.

Ragnars saga loðbrókar. In *Vǫlsunga saga ok Ragnars saga loðbrókar* 1906–08. Ed. M. Olsen.
Rowe, Elizabeth Ashman 2008. '*Ragnars saga loðbrókar, Ragnars þáttr*, and the Political World of Haukr Erlendsson'. In *Fornaldarsagaerne: Myter og virkelighed*. Ed. Agneta Ney, Ármann Jakobsson and Annette Lassen, 347–78.
Rowe, Elizabeth Ashman forthcoming. *Ragnarr loðbrók in Medieval Icelandic Historiography*.
Shippey, T. A. 1998. '"The Death-Song of Ragnar Lodbrog": A Study in Sensibilities'. In *Medievalism in the Modern World: Essays in Honour of Leslie J. Workman*. Ed. R. Utz and T. A. Shippey, 155–72.
Torfi Tulinius 2003. 'Fornaldarsaga och ideologi: Tillbaka till "The Matter of the North"'. In *Fornaldarsagornas struktur och ideologi*. Ed. Ármann Jakobsson, Annette Lassen, Agneta Ney, 73–88.
de Vries, Jan 1923. 'Die historischen Grundlagen der Ragnarssaga loðbrókar'. *Arkiv för nordisk filologi* 39, 244–74.
Vǫlsunga saga. In *Vǫlsunga saga ok Ragnars saga loðbrókar* 1906–08. Ed. M. Olsen.
Watkins, Calvert 1995. *How to Kill a Dragon: Aspects of Indo-European Poetics*.
Yngvars saga víðfǫrla 1910. Ed. E. Olson.

HYGGIN OK FORSJÁL. WISDOM AND WOMEN'S COUNSEL IN HRÓLFS SAGA GAUTREKSSONAR

JÓHANNA KATRÍN FRIÐRIKSDÓTTIR

It is well known that in the nineteenth century, and in some cases well into the twentieth century, the *fornaldarsögur* were generally considered to have little value other than for philological and comparative purposes, and many earlier critics argued that these sagas were intended to entertain rather than edify. Scholarship on *Hrólfs saga Gautrekssonar* is no exception; in the introduction to his edition of the saga, Ferdinand Detter described it as a compilation of episodes under a common title, devoid of aesthetic merit: 'Ästhetischen Werth hat natürlich diese Compilation, welche unter dem Titel Hrólfssaga Gautrekssonar überliefert ist, nicht' (Detter 1891, xli), and as recently as 2009, the saga was described by one scholar as 'fiction pure and simple, [whose] purpose is entirely frivolous' (Chesnutt 2009, 96–97). Hermann Pálsson and Paul Edwards were among the first scholars to treat the saga as a text of literary merit, describing it as 'a study in moderation and excess' (Hermann Pálsson and Edwards 1971, 42). A hundred years after Detter, Marianne Kalinke, who has produced the most sustained study of *Hrólfs saga*, characterised the saga as the 'acme of Icelandic bridal-quest romance', a type of narrative in which the wooing and securing of a wife is the determinant of the plot and has the greatest impact on the hero's actions (Kalinke 1990, 25). Kalinke argues that *Hrólfs saga* is no compilation but a unified text consisting of four consecutive bridal quests, each involving different obstacles for the suitors to conquer, and that every episode, even apparent digressions unconnected to the main plot, has a purpose in the overall structure of the saga (Kalinke 1990, ch. 2, esp. 50–52). Both Kalinke and Torfi Tulinius praise the work's structural sophistication and the author's masterful handling of the many layers of subplot, the use of a wide range of literary motifs and the portrait of Hrólfr, the protagonist and ideal hero. Attempting to place the saga in an historical context, Tulinius maintains that the idea of a virtuous prince being favoured as king over his older but less impressive brother would have had currency with the Sturlungar clan in the thirteenth century, who several times during that age had a younger brother as their leader. He also sees it as generally perpetuating the ideology of royal authority in times of political turmoil, in particular after Iceland became subject to the Norwegian monarchy in 1262 (2002, 172–73). Simultaneously, as both these scholars have observed, the saga also deals with the problems of marriage and upward social mobility, as Tulinius has argued, in a comic mode (Kalinke 39, 67; Tulinius 174–76). The saga's sheer variety and originality in employing a wide range of foreign and native motifs and sophisticated narrative techniques marks it out from many of the more formulaic legendary texts, and the author's obvious aim to edify by promoting certain virtues, as well as the intricate structure and carefully crafted characters, reveal an ambition for the text to surpass 'mere' entertainment.

The importance of wisdom in *Hrólfs saga Gautrekssonar* has been noted before: Tulinius lists wisdom among the many virtues that define Hrólfr as the 'ideal king' (Tulinius 170–71), Kalinke observes on several occasions that female characters are wise or prudent (Kalinke 1990, 29, 47, 59), and Pálsson and Edwards stress the role of 'wise counsellors' (Hermann Pálsson and Edwards 1972, 12). Nevertheless, more remains to be said about the nature of wisdom as it is conceived in this saga, and how the author communicates wisdom to the audience through female characters, juxtaposing them with less wise males. Again and again, male characters are depicted as rash and impulsive, susceptible to the influence of gossiping courtiers and keen on using force and violence rather than diplomacy, while women often manage to sway conflicts towards peaceful resolution by giving their husbands carefully selected pieces of advice on how to act. The wise hero Hrólfr rises above this behaviour but he is not altogether as virtuous a ruler as he has been represented, for example by Tulinius (170); until his wife intervenes, Hrólfr is unwilling to follow the behaviour expected of kings, such as keeping oaths and rewarding his followers with mutual loyalty. As I will argue, in *Hrólfs saga Gautrekssonar* the role of counsellor is gendered as female, but the content of women's counsel is universal; it essentially revolves around adhering to social mores and being prudent, that is to say, showing forethought, caution and sound judgement in all matters.

Texts and content of Hrólfs saga Gautrekssonar

Hrólfs saga Gautrekssonar is preserved in more than sixty manuscripts.[1] The earliest is AM 567 XIV 4to ß, a fragment dated to around 1300; this is most likely the oldest extant manuscript of a *fornaldarsaga* (Guðni

---

[1] For a full list of manuscripts, editions, translations, *rímur* and secondary literature, see Driscoll and Hufnagel 2008.

Jónsson 1944, vii) and gives a *terminus ante quem* for the saga's date of composition, which has been placed in the late thirteenth century (Hollander 1912). The saga exists in two redactions, both medieval: a shorter and perhaps older version (represented by Stockholm Perg. 4to no. 7), and a somewhat longer and more frequently edited version (represented by AM 152 fol. and AM 590 b–c, 4to), the basis for my interpretation in this essay.[2] The somewhat different narrative of the shorter redaction diverges in several interesting details, but space does not allow a comparison of the versions.

At the beginning of the saga two Scandinavian kings, Gautrekr and Hringr, who have been close friends for years, become suspicious of each other, and each contemplates whether he should be the first to strike. Their apprehension is caused by slander and gossip in the hall (50–51):

> Höfðu þeir jafnan verit báðir saman í hernaði, meðan þeir váru yngri, ok skildu aldri sína vináttu, meðan þeir fundust jafnliga, en nú tók heldr at greinast af meðalgöngu vándra manna, þeira er róg kveyktu í millum þeira. Kom þá svá, at hvárrtveggi bjóst at stríða hvárr við annan.

> They had usually fought together when they were younger, and as long as they saw each other often their friendship never faltered, but at this time it began to fail as the result of the interference of evil men who spread slander between them. It reached the point where each of them prepared for war against the other.

Fortunately, Gautrekr and Hringr's queens intervene before it comes to battle, and both women successfully advise their husbands to keep the peace. The kings remain friends and their sons, Ingjaldr and the protagonist Hrólfr, who is fostered by Hringr, become sworn brothers. Hrólfr, although a younger brother, is deemed worthier of ascending the throne when his father dies, since he surpasses all other men in both physical and mental qualities. Encouraged by his older brother Ketill, King Hrólfr sets out to find a suitable wife. He ambitiously decides to woo the maiden-king Þornbjörg, a princess who calls herself King Þórbergr (a masculine name), dresses in armour, jousts, fights with swords and

---

[2] Unless otherwise stated, references are to *Hrólfs saga Gautrekssonar* 1944, which is also reprinted (minus the introduction) in vol. IV of Guðni Jónsson's four-volume Íslendingasagnaútgáfan collection of *fornaldarsögur*, published in 1950. This edition (based on C. C. Rafn's 1830 edition) follows AM 152 fol. (*c.*1500–25) and its copy, AM 590 b–c, 4to (17th century). Another version of the saga is edited by Ferdinand Detter after the Stockholm. Perg. 7 4to (*c.*1300–25) in *Hrólfs saga Gautrekssonar* 1891. Translations from the saga are my own unless otherwise indicated.

keeps her own court, ruling a third of Sweden.[3] Hrólfr is first forcefully rejected, conquered in battle and humiliated by the maiden-king and his/her army, but after his second attack, Hrólfr outdoes Þornbjörg, they marry and she turns to feminine behaviour and activities such as embroidery. After a second bridal quest to Russia, which Hrólfr reluctantly undertakes with his brother Ketill at the urging of Queen Þornbjörg, Hrólfr and his companions travel to England, where they dwell at the court of King Ella. The two kings become close but their friendship is tested when there is ill-will towards Hrólfr among some of the courtiers, who slander him to Ella, as well as luring him into fighting, somewhat surprisingly, a lion. In this English episode Hrólfr's depiction as a wise and cautious hero, who deserves his success and the audience's sympathy, is reaffirmed. The final and most dangerous bridal quest, to find a wife for one of Hrólfr's supporters, takes him to Ireland, where the bride's hostile father nearly defeats the Scandinavians. In this episode two noblewomen are instrumental in averting disaster: the bride Ingibjörg, whose cunning tricks are intended to help Hrólfr's army subvert her father's authority, and the resourceful Þornbjörg, who once again takes up sword and armour, travels to Ireland and helps her husband and his men triumph over their adversary. The saga ends with all the remaining unmarried characters being paired up, and the author's metafictional comment to those who dispute the veracity of the saga (151): *Hvárt sem satt er eða eigi, þá hafi sá gaman af, er þat má at verða, en hinir leiti annars þess gamans, er þeim þykkir betra* 'But whether it's true or not, let those enjoy the story who can, while those who can't had better look for some other amusement' (Hermann Pálsson and Edwards, 1972, 148).

Women, Wisdom and Counsel

The most important female virtues in *Hrólfs saga* are explicitly stated to be prudence and foresight. When Ketill urges his brother Hrólfr to marry, his requirements for the wife's qualities are twofold, that the bride should be of royal birth and *hyggin ok forsjál* (58–59):[4]

> Þú ert maðr ókvæntr, ok mundir þú þykkja miklu gildari konungr, ef þú fengir þér kvánfang við þitt hæfi . . . Þá mundi yðar sæmd vaxa, ef þér bæðið þeirar konungsdóttur, er bæði er hyggin ok forsjál.

---

[3] In the shorter version, the princess is named Þórbjörg and she does not adopt a masculine name.

[4] These reflections are missing from the shorter redaction of the saga.

You are an unmarried man, and you would be considered a much more powerful king if you found a suitable wife... Your honour would prosper if you proposed to a princess who had both prudence and foresight.

Later King Hringr's wife advises her husband against waging war on his friend King Gautrekr, mentioning Gautrekr's acquisition of a wise and excellent wife as one of the arguments for keeping the peace (51): *Hefir hann fengit svá vitra konu ok góðfúsa, at allan ykkarn félagsskap mun hún saman draga ok í lag færa þat, sem áfátt er* 'He has acquired such a wise and benevolent wife that she will bring you back together and put right what has gone amiss in your friendship'. Furthermore, when Þornbjörg relinquishes her status as a maiden-king and marries Hrólfr, the narrator informs us that she is, among many other things, *vitr ok vinsæl, málsnjöll ok spakráðug* 'wise and beloved by many, eloquent and wise of counsel' (84). It is striking that traditional female attributes such as beauty are nowhere mentioned; noble lineage and intelligence are the only criteria against which a prospective wife is to be measured. As it turns out, female wisdom continues to be held in esteem: Þornbjörg, Hrólfr's wife, is wise like all the other prominent women in the saga, and all play an important part in their husbands' lives, often preventing them from acting rashly and imprudently.

The association of women with wisdom, knowledge and good counsel is by no means unique to *Hrólfs saga Gautrekssonar* or the *fornaldarsögur*; many such examples can be found in Old Norse literature. Unnr djúpúðga in *Laxdæla saga* is, as her epithet 'deep-minded' and description as *afbragð annarra kvenna* 'superior to all other women' indicates, a figure of surpassing wisdom, advising her deferential family members on various matters until her death from old age. Brynhildr Buðladóttir is also exceptionally wise; this is stressed throughout *Vǫlsunga saga*, where Sigurðr Fáfnisbani at one point declares her the wisest woman in the world (*Vǫlsunga saga* 54), and in the Eddic poem *Sigrdrífumál* the valkyrie Sigrdrífa, often identified with Brynhildr owing to the conflation of the two in *Vǫlsunga saga*, provides Sigurðr with the important gnomic wisdom and rune-knowledge which all heroes need. The gnomic poem *Hávamál* portrays women as *horscar* 'wise' when it advises men on how to seduce them by flattery and deception (st. 91):

> þá vér fegrst mælom,   er vér flást hyggiom,
>   þat tælir horsca hugi.

> when we speak most fairly, then we think most falsely,
>   that entraps the wise mind.

In the same poem *Billings mær*, described with epithets such as *iþ ráð-spaka* 'sagacious woman' (st. 102) and *in horsca mær* 'wise girl' (st. 96), shows wisdom, tact and resourcefulness in eluding Óðinn's advances.[5] Even as far back as the late first century AD, in Tacitus's *Germania*, women are connected with wisdom and counsel, while men pay great heed to their advice: '[the Germans] believe that there resides in women an element of holiness and a gift of prophecy; and so they do not scorn to ask their advice, or lightly disregard their replies' (Tacitus 1970, 108). The same idea appears in Old English texts; *Maxims I* asserts that it is fitting for a queen to provide counsel to her king, *him ræd witan / boldagendum bæm ætsomne* 'she should give him advice, both of them together ruling over the fortress' (ll. 21b–22), and *Beowulf* reflects this idea in the roles of the queens Wealhþeow and Hygd. Thus there is an attested and ancient tradition associating women with wisdom and advice in Germanic culture.

It is a commonplace in the *fornaldarsögur* to describe women with the epithet *væn ok vitr* 'beautiful/promising and wise' (or variants thereof), and these sagas almost universally feature women, mainly of noble descent, as wise figures dispensing beneficial advice to their male kin; the equally traditional figure of the woman inciting to vengeance is in fact rare in the *fornaldarsögur*.[6] Women also engage in activities which show their intelligence, interpreting dreams and healing wounds, and some of them possess knowledge which can be related to certain conventionally masculine *íþróttir*, such as academic learning (e.g. astrology) and playing chess.[7] Most importantly, women are expected to share their wisdom and men sometimes actively seek their counsel: dispensing advice is a socially sanctioned role for women and plays an integral part in *Hrólfs saga*.[8] Women's advice is not listed in a catalogue in the manner of the Eddic poems or the six specific rules of conduct which king Hǫfundr gives to his son Heiðrekr in *Hervarar saga ok Heiðreks*, but is rather tailored to specific situations; thus it has an apparent *ad hoc* quality. However, certain universal themes emerge from this advice, themes which can arguably

---

[5] References are to *Hávamál* (1962). Translations are from 'Sayings of the High One', Larrington 1996, pp. 14–38.

[6] Marsibil Hálfdanardóttir in *Sǫrla saga sterka* is a notable exception, as are the female characters in *Vǫlsunga saga* and *Ragnars saga loðbrókar*.

[7] See e.g. Hervör and Díana in *Hjálmþés saga ok Ölvis*.

[8] Hrólfr asks his wife what she thinks about his forthcoming bridal quest to Russia (94) and for advice on how to proceed with the bridal quest to Ireland (115), and Eirekr asks his wife for advice on how to receive Hrólfr (64).

be found elsewhere in Old Norse wisdom poetry such as *Hugsvinnsmál*, an Old Norse translation of the Latin gnomic poem *Disticha Catonis*, as well as the more famous *Hávamál*, which values the woman as faithful confidante, *eyrarúna* (Larrington 1993, 52).[9] These themes, such as loyalty, upholding oaths and showing hospitality, relate to social conduct, and they stress prudence and moderation. In what follows, I will give a few examples to illustrate each of the following themes: foresight, loyalty, caution and hospitality.

In the first bridal quest of the saga, the bride, Ingibjörg, is wooed by two men, both kings: the ageing Gautrekr and the strapping young Ólafr. Her father allows her to choose which suitor to marry and Ingibjörg, in a long monologue, first takes care to flatter both men but then explains her reasons for choosing the older Gautrekr with a metaphor, comparing the younger king to an apple tree with great potential for producing a good crop, but not yet attested (47).[10] King Gautrekr, however, is like an apple tree in full bloom; it has plenty of branches and already many kinds of apples, or in other words, he has already proven himself as a distinguished ruler and is therefore the more reliable option. Ingibjörg's decision demonstrates her *forsjálni* 'foresight' and is fruitful; Ólafr is outraged at his rejection and attacks Gautrekr, who boldly kills his aggressor along with his entire force, showing his superiority despite his old age. Thus from the very beginning of the saga, the narrator establishes that female characters possess mental qualities, such as foresight, which allow them to perceive what is the most prudent course of action to take. *Hugsvinnsmál* also emphasises this quality, advising that one should consider every matter thoroughly and use caution, discernment and foresight (st. 81):

> Um lítaz   þarf maðr á alla vegu
>   ok við villu varaz;
> glöggþekkinn   skyldi gumna hverr
>   ok fróðr ok forsjáll vera.

A man has to look around in all directions and beware of falsehood; every man should be clear-sighted and wise and foresighted.

Hávamál (especially sts 58–60) stresses foresight as well, albeit more pragmatically; it recommends being prepared in advance, whether with provisions and housing or ensuring supporters at the assembly, so as to

---

[9] References to and translations of *Hugsvinnsmál* are from *Hugsvinnsmál* 2007.
[10] According to Kalinke (1990, 74, n. 10), the apple-tree motif is biblical, originally deriving from the *Song of Songs*, 2.3.

anticipate problems.[11] In *Hrólfs saga*, Ingibjörg's foresight in picking Gautrekr as her husband results in the continuation of his lineage and the birth of the saga's outstanding hero, Hrólfr.

Ingibjörg and Gautrekr's marriage is a happy one and we next hear of them ten years later, when trouble starts brewing between Gautrekr and his Danish friend King Hringr. Ingibjörg and Hringr's wife must talk sense into their husbands when each king becomes suspicious of the other's alleged evil intentions. These suspicions are based on hearsay and rumours at court rather than facts, as both queens point out, and Hringr's wife chastises her husband for speaking *ókonungliga* 'not in a kingly way' and *óvitrliga* 'unwisely', similar to the expressions used by Ingibjörg to Gautrekr (52). In long speeches, the women urge their husbands not to pay any attention to the slander, *rógr*, of wicked men or do each other harm, but instead persuade them to honour their friendship and bond. The wise and sensible words of Hringr's wife are (51):

> Ger svá vel, herra, at eigi finnist í þínu brjósti sú greymennska, at þér vilið svá niðr fella ok undir fótum troða svá marga góða hluti sem hvárr ykkar hefir við annan gert. Haldið, herra, við Gautrek konung með prýði ok drengskap uppteknum góðvilja með ást ok fullkomnum friði, ok týn eigi fyrir vándra manna orðróm svá góðs manns vináttu.
>
> Please, my lord, do not let be found in your heart such paltriness that you will pull down and trample on the many good things that each of you has done for the other. My lord, stay true to King Gautrekr, uphold bravely and nobly your past goodwill, with affection and peace, and do not lose the friendship of such a good man because of the gossip of wicked people.

These words are loaded indeed, the word *greymennska* conveying the forcefulness of the queen's argument, comparing the king to a lowly dog if he breaks his vows. Furthermore, the phrase *undir fótum troða* 'to trample on' metaphorically condemns the arrogance, disloyalty and recklessness of Hringr's mooted betrayal of his friend. Several instances of alliteration and couplets emphasise the words in question, a method used in both wisdom poetry and curses. Clearly this advice, which promotes peace and loyalty, is to be taken seriously; the outcome is that instead of warring, the kings remain friends and Hringr nobly offers to foster Gautrekr's son, Hrólfr.

Hrólfr's wife, the former maiden-king Þornbjörg Eireksdóttir, is another example of a wise queen. After their wedding she does not become the passive and conformist opposite of what she was before.

---

[11] For discussion, see Larrington 1993, 37–38.

Rather, although no longer masquerading as a man, she participates actively in matters of state and gives her husband advice, both on her own initiative and at his request. Þornbjörg is strikingly independent: when Hrólfr is in trouble in Ireland on one of his several missions, she first dispatches his servant Þórir to help him, and then summons an army, once again dons her armour and sets off to find her husband and his companions (139):

> Drottning dró ok her saman af Svíþjóð. Tók hún þá skjöld ok sverð ok réðst til ferðar með Gautreki, syni sínum . . . Ok í ákveðnum stað fundust þau öll saman [drottning, Ketill ok Ingjaldr] með miklu liði. Hafði drottning ráð ok skipan fyrir liði þeira.

> The queen summoned an army in Sweden. Then she took shield and sword and set out with her son, Gautrekr . . . And at the appointed place they all met [the queen, Ketill and Ingjaldr] with a great force. The queen commanded their army.

Although she transgresses the traditional female gender role by taking military action, she is not stigmatised by it.

The essence of Queen Þornbjörg's advice to her husband is to be loyal to his supporters and observe social customs, and she entreats him several times to support his brother and sworn brother in their endeavours, while Hrólfr himself had planned to stay at home. Her response to his refusal to help his sworn brother Ásmundr woo the princess of Ireland is highly critical (114):

> Þat gerir þú illa, því at eigi veit ek þann mann, attu ættir heldr sæmdar at leita en honum. Hefir hann yðr lengi vel fylgt ok þjónat kurteisliga ok verit með yðr í margri hreystiferð ok þolat með yðr bæði blítt ok strítt ok reynzt jafnan inn vaskasti maðr.

> That is a bad thing to do, as I do not know of any man to whom you should rather do honour than him. He has been your loyal follower for a long time and served you courteously and been by your side in many a bold expedition and endured with you both good times and bad and always proved to be the most valiant of men.

Thus Þornbjörg reproaches her husband for his reluctance to help someone who has served him well, and reminds him of his duty to his retainer. The adjective *kurteislega* 'courteously' evokes chivalric values, including decorum, valour and duty to one's lord, and the reciprocality of the lord-retainer relationship is highlighted: the *dróttinn* 'master, lord' must choose his friends carefully and be loyal to them, just as they are to him. Loyalty is also emphasised by the third bride, princess Álöf of Russia, who quarrels with her foster-father Þórir because of his refusal to help the king in fighting the Scandinavians who have come to woo her: '*Mun þér þetta ok til mikils ódrengskapar virt, þar sem þú ert hans öndugismaðr ok þegit af honum margar gjafir ok ráðit einn með honum öllu því, sem þú vildir*' "This will be considered exceedingly dishonourable of you, as you are his right-hand man and you have received many gifts from him and you alone have been able to counsel him in every matter you pleased" (106). Thus we find examples of both lords and retainers needing a considerable amount of persuasion before they do what duty and honour demand of them.

Hávamál articulates the same ideas about the reciprocal nature of (homo) social bonds. The poem stresses loyalty and generosity to one's friends (sts 42, 44):

> Vin sínom   scal maðr vinr vera
>   ok gialda giǫf við giǫf;
> hlátr við hlátri   skyli hǫlðar taca,
>   enn lausung við lygi.
>
>   . . .
>
> Veiztu, ef þú vin átt,   þannz þú illa trúir,
>   oc vill þú af hánom gott geta:
> geði scaltu við þann blanda   ok giǫfom scipta,
>   fara at finna opt.

> To his friends a man should be a friend
> and repay gifts with gifts;
> laughter a man should give for laughter
> And repay treachery with lies.

> You know, if you've a friend whom you really trust
> and from whom you want nothing but good,
> you should mix your soul with his and exchange gifts,
> go and see him often.

The friendship described in these strophes embraces not only the material exchange of gifts and visits, but also the figurative repaying of laughter with laughter and 'mix[ing] your soul with his', or as Carolyne Larrington observes, mutual emotional attention and intellectual engagement between friends (1993, 32). In the same spirit, the narrator suggests that mutual mistrust only arises between Hringr and Gautrekr after they stop seeing each other regularly (*skildu aldri sína vináttu, meðan þeir fundust jafnliga* 'their friendship never faltered as long as they saw each other often') and Hringr's queen suggests a visit to Gautland to improve the relationship with Gautrekr (51–52). Women in the saga thus echo the teachings of *Há-*

vamál, encouraging their husbands to honour their homosocial bonds in all appropriate and customary forms, remain loyal to their friends and allies and not to set store by idle talk and hearsay; in short, to display prudence, moderation and loyalty.

In the example of the two queens of Hringr and Gautrekr (discussed above), female speech is coded as positive and wise, stressing the importance of deliberation, moderation and caution, and it is depicted as directly opposite to both the malicious gossip of the (presumably) male retainers and the kings' foolish impulse to believe this talk and act on it. What C. Stephen Jaeger refers to as the 'miseries of courtiers', an historical reality to some extent, reflects this literary motif of negative male talk at court (1985, 58–64); compare from the *Íslendingasögur* the Hildiríðarsynir's slander of Þórólfr in *Egils saga Skalla-Grímssonar* (*Egils saga* 29–33). Competition between rulers' followers could lead to treachery and backstabbing; intrigue, plotting and manipulation of the king, the opposite of courtly virtues, were common strategies in the pursuit of power at medieval courts. Women warn against trusting the words of the king's men. When a similar situation involving male gossip in the hall arises later in the saga during Hrólfr's sojourn in England, the author seems to offer a counter-example in order to show how a wise king *should* act, without prompting from his wife. In this episode, King Ella's noblemen initiate a smear campaign against Hrólfr, and the English king tricks everyone into thinking that he is paying attention to their words and intends to kill Hrólfr. However, it soon emerges that both kings, instead of becoming suspicious and distrustful of one another, have acted prudently and remained loyal. Here, they do not need to be recalled to proper behaviour by their wives as they, and the audience, have already learned the lesson of caution and loyalty. This episode reaffirms the point by showing what happens when one acts prudently.

This attitude to sinister talk recalls the advice of *Hávamál* about caution and wariness, and of untrustworthy people, *ill ráð hefir maðr opt þegit / annars brióstom ór* 'one has often received bad advice from another's heart' (st. 9), as well as *Hugsvinnsmál*'s warning against backbiters (st. 74):

> Sögvísum manni skaltu sjaldan trúa,
> þeim er með rógi rennr,
> þvít málugra manns reynaz margar sögur
> lýða kind at lygi.

You must seldom believe a tattling man who runs with slander, because many stories of a talkative man prove to be lies for the race of men.

These positively-coded speech acts also evoke the *hvöt* 'incitement speech', or rather its absence, contrasting sharply with the negative attitude to female speech in some of the *Íslendingasögur*. In this genre, as Helga Kress has argued, women are often the spreaders of gossip (1991, 130–56). The malicious male-coded talk in the hall highlights women's extremely positive role in *Hrólfs saga*.

Early on in *Hrólfs saga*, Queen Ingigerðr, the wife of King Eirekr of Sweden, has a premonitory dream of Hrólfr's arrival and his intention to propose to their daughter Þornbjörg. The king asks for her advice on how to receive him, and she encourages her husband to show him honour, explaining that she doubts that their daughter will receive a marriage proposal from anyone worthier than the impressive Hrólfr (64):

> Vel skulu þér taka Hrólfi konungi, ef hann sækir yðr heim, ok sýna honum ina mestu blíðu, því at hann er inn mesti afreksmaðr um marga hluti ok eigi víst, at yðar dóttir fái frægra mann en sem mér er hann sagðr.
>
> Receive King Hrólfr well if he visits you, and show him the utmost kindness, for he is an outstanding man in many respects and it is by no means certain that your daughter will get a more renowned husband, judging from how he has been described to me.

The first four stanzas of *Hávamál* also deal with the arrival of a guest and although caution is advised towards a newcomer, there is more emphasis on the proper treatment of visitors, giving them what they need, such as an appropriate seat, warmth, nourishment, clothing and a warm welcome. King Eirekr, however, follows neither this code of conduct nor his wife's advice, since he considers Hrólfr's social status, as the king of a much smaller and less powerful kingdom (Gautland), well below his own; instead, he mocks Hrólfr, offering him and his men one month's stay as a charity to their impoverished army. The queen is not pleased when she hears of the scorn with which Hrólfr has been treated and reproaches the king. The next day Eirekr is more generous to his guest and eventually he gives his blessing to Hrólfr's proposal to Þornbjörg.

As mentioned earlier, Hrólfr goes on to win Þornbjörg and the marriage is a happy one. The queen's motivation for encouraging her husband to treat Hrólfr well after the king had initially slighted him is intriguing, as she is less concerned with Hrólfr's outstanding attributes than with foreign politics, or to be precise, his connections to his foster-father, King Hringr. She tells her husband (67), ek vil, at þér vægið fyrir Hrólfi konungi í orðum, því at . . . þér mun verða þungt at etja við hann þrái eða kappi, því at hann hefir styrk af Danakonungi, því at hann ræðr öllu með Hringi konungi, fóstra sínum.

I want you to yield to King Hrólfr, as it will be difficult for you to match your force against his, for he has the support of the King of Denmark and keeps close counsel with his foster-father Hringr.

Thus hospitality, an ancient Germanic social obligation which should be fulfilled on principle, has, according to the queen, an additional strategic payoff in this context. It is noteworthy that the queen's involvement in the kingdom's foreign policy and knowledge of the finer details of neighbouring countries' politics confirms her advisory role in the public sphere and thus suggests that she has some degree of legitimate authority.

The Function of Women's Counsel

The motivation of female characters who dispense advice is usually presented as being either to resolve problems before they lead to violence or, if physical conflict has already taken place, to put an end to it. The wise female character is a vessel and mouthpiece for 'good' or 'positive' values which promote peace and stability. This could have originated before the adoption of Christianity, the result of Christian influence or ideas imported with romance literature. Just as the source and date of composition of *Hávamál*, and whether it belongs to the pagan or post-conversion Christian period, is contested, so the origin of the tradition of women's pacific counsel is unclear; Theodore Andersson notes that 'the concept of moderation is older than Christianity' (1989, 69).[12] The advice frequently serves a narrative function, foreshadowing events and heightening the audience's anticipation without ruining the suspense until the end, when we see how the hero fares. The advice-giver's role is gendered, and women are permitted, even expected, to give advice to men in various situations, usually with the purpose of moderating a planned outcome and preventing and/or averting threats to personal or national safety. Women's counsel is usually followed to the hero's advantage, proving to be socially attuned and effective. The content of the advice is widely useful, revolving around social behaviour, such as discounting unfounded rumours and upholding one's duties and responsibilities towards family and sworn brothers, guarding against those with bad intentions, but also not prejudging people and showing them hospitality regardless

---

[12] For discussion on the dating and origin of *Hávamál*, see e.g. Larrington 1993, 16–17.

of social status. In *Hrólfs saga Gautrekssonar*, women and men are contrasted: the women are wise and the men less so. The exceptions are the kings Hrólfr and Ella, who are indeed portrayed as virtuous, especially Hrólfr, whose wisdom and caution are among his most important qualities, despite his initial refusal to help his loyal sworn brother in his mission to acquire a bride. Thus perhaps the ultimate sign of Hrólfr's wisdom is that he takes counsel from his wife instead of unswervingly believing in his own superiority.

Conclusion

Hávamál includes a warning against the fickleness of women (st. 84):

> Meyiar orðom   scyli manngi trúa,
>   né því er qveðr kona;
> þvíat á hverfanda hvéli   vóro þeim hiǫrto skǫpuð,
>   brigð í brióst um lagit.

> The words of a girl no one should trust,
> nor what a woman says;
> for on a whirling wheel their hearts were made,
> deceit lodged in their breasts.

This strophe echoes the warnings that appear in st. 91, cited above, where men are said to be equally untrustworthy in their efforts to seduce women. The idea of women's fickle and deceitful nature cannot have had a universal currency in medieval Iceland since the authors of sagas such as *Hrólfs saga Gautrekssonar* deliberately use women's counsel as a literary means to champion prudence, loyalty, honour, moderation and caution, much as *Hávamál* does. Women's counsel aims at maintaining the *status quo*, promoting peace and social cohesion rather than warfare and strife or women's independent agendas. Since the advice is normally dispensed to husbands (rather than brothers and fathers), it signals woman's position in society as primarily that of loyal wife. Despite being deployed in specific situations, female advice always has a broader relevance; lessons drawn from it benefit not only the hero, but in a larger social context, everyone in the saga audience. The troubled social and historical circumstances in which texts such as *Hrólfs saga Gautrekssonar* emerge perhaps indicate that the preoccupation with and promotion of these values reflects their authors' rejection of their opposites: excess, greed, recklessness, selfishness and disloyalty.

Bibliography

Andersson, Theodore M. 1989. 'The Displacement of the Heroic Ideal in the Family Sagas'. In *Sagas of the Icelanders. A Book of Essays*. Ed. John Tucker, 40–70.
Brennu-Njáls saga 1954. Ed. Einar Ól. Sveinsson. Íslenzk fornrit XII.
Chesnutt, Michael 2009. 'The Content and Meaning of *Gjafa-Refs saga*'. In *Fornaldarsagaerne. Myter og virkilighed. Studier i de oldislandske fornaldarsögur Norðurlanda*. Eds. Agneta Ney, Ármann Jakobsson and Annette Lassen.
Driscoll, M. J. and Silvia Hufnagel 2008. 'Hrólfs saga Gautrekssonar (2 versions)'. In *Fornaldarsögur norðurlanda: A bibliography of manuscripts, editions, translations and secondary literature*. http://www.am-dk.net/fas/hsg.html. Accessed February 2, 2009.
Egils saga Skalla-Grímssonar 1933. Ed. Sigurður Nordal. Íslenzk fornrit II.
Guðni Jónsson 1944. 'Formáli'. In *Fornaldarsögur norðurlanda* III. Ed. Guðni Jónsson and Bjarni Vilhjálmsson.
Hávamál 1962. In *Edda. Die Lieder des Codex Regius nebst verwandten Denkmälern*. 4th ed. Ed. Gustav Neckel, rev. Hans Kuhn.
Helga Kress 1991. 'Staðlausir stafir. Um slúður sem uppsprettu frásagnar í Íslendingasögum'. *Skírnir* 165, 130–56.
Hermann Pálsson and Paul Edwards 1971. *Legendary Fiction in Medieval Iceland*. Studia Islandica 30.
Hermann Pálsson and Paul Edwards, trans., 1972. *Hrolf Gautreksson. A Viking Romance*.
Hollander, Lee M. 1913. 'The Relative Age of the Gautrekssaga and the Hrólfssaga Gautrekssonar'. *Arkiv för nordisk filologi* 29, 120–34.
Hollander, Lee M. 1912. 'The Gautland Cycle of Sagas'. *Journal of English and Germanic Philology* 11, 61–81, 209–17.
Hrólfs saga Gautrekssonar 1944. In *Fornaldarsögur norðurlanda* III. Ed. Guðni Jónsson and Bjarni Vilhjálmsson.
Hrólfssaga Gautrekssonar 1891. In *Zwei Fornaldarsögur: Hrólfssaga Gautrekssonar und Ásmundarsaga kappabana; nach Cod. Holm. 7, 4to*. Ed. Ferdinand Detter.
Hugsvinnsmál 2007. Ed. Tarrin Wills and Stefanie Würth. In *Poetry on Christian Subjects*. Skaldic Poetry of the Scandinavian Middle Ages 7. Ed. Margaret Clunies Ross, 358–449.
Jaeger, C. Stephen 1985. *The Origins of Courtliness. Civilizing Trends and the Formation of Courtly Ideals 939–1210*.
Kalinke, Marianne 1986. 'The Misogamous Maiden Kings of Icelandic Romance'. *Scripta Islandica* 37, 47–71.
Kalinke, Marianne 1990. *Bridal-Quest Romance in Medieval Iceland*. Islandica XLVI.
Kalinke, Marianne (forthcoming). '*Clári saga, Hrólfs saga Gautrekssonar*, and the Evolution of Icelandic Romance'.
Larrington, Carolyne 1993. *A Store of Common Sense. Gnomic Theme and Style in Old Icelandic and Old English Wisdom Poetry*.
Larrington, Carolyne, trans., 1996. *The Poetic Edda*.
Laxdœla saga 1934. Ed. Einar Ól. Sveinsson. Íslenzk fornrit V.

Tacitus 1970. *The Agricola and the Germania*. Trans. H. Mattingly. Rev. S. A. Handford.

Tulinius, Torfi H. 2002. *The Matter of the North. The Rise of Literary Fiction in Thirteenth-Century Iceland*. Trans. Randi C. Eldevik.

Tulinius, Torfi H. 2005. 'Sagas of Icelandic Prehistory (*fornaldarsögur*)'. In *A Companion to Old Norse-Icelandic Literature and Culture*. Ed. Rory McTurk, 447–61.

Vǫlsunga saga. In *Vǫlsunga saga ok Ragnars saga loðbrókar* 1906–08. Ed. Magnus Olsen.

VIÐ ÞIK SÆTTUMSK EK ALDRI. ǪRVAR-ODDS SAGA AND THE MEANINGS OF ǪGMUNDR EYÞJÓFSBANI

MARTIN ARNOLD

It is widely acknowledged that *Ǫrvar-Odds saga* is one of the oldest and was one of the most popular of the *fornaldarsögur*. The saga cannot, however, be considered a single unified work, as there are marked differences between the narratives of the early and late manuscript groups. The earliest redactions are those given in the fourteenth-century S and slightly younger M manuscripts (respectively, Stock. Perg. 7 4to and AM 344a 4to), both of which derive independently from a lost thirteenth-century original. Of most interest among the later redactions are those given in the fifteenth-century manuscripts assigned as A and B (respectively, AM 343 4to and AM 471 4to). The chronology of the various manuscripts, actual and deduced, was established by R. C. Boer in 1888 (see Appendix for the manuscript stemma). This essay follows Boer's transcriptions of the S, M and A redactions, in which M can be regarded, to some extent, as an intermediary between S and A.[1] Of these, the A redaction is probably the best known, as it is this version of the saga that is given in Guðni Jónsson's collection *Fornaldar sögur norðurlanda* (*Örvar-Odds saga* 1954), and translated into English by Paul Edwards and Hermann Pálsson as *Arrow-Odd: A Medieval Novel* (1970) (published again in the anthology *Seven Viking Romances* (1985, 25–137)). Characterising this younger redaction and its contemporaries and descendants are substantial interpolations of a fantastical nature which significantly shift the narrative focus of the oldest redactions and, as a result, alter the saga's overall dynamic and possible meaning.

Elements of the basic tale of Ǫrvar-Oddr as told in the early redactions would appear, at least in part, to derive from oral traditions. This is apparent from references to the hero in twelfth- and early thirteenth-century sources. Saxo Grammaticus's *Gesta Danorum* mentions Oddr as the Viking warrior Arvaroddus in the struggle against the berserk Anganterus and his brothers on the island of Samsø/Sámsey (Book 5). Oddr is also

---

[1] Quotations from the S and M redactions are taken from R. C. Boer's edition (*Ǫrvar-Odds saga* 1888). Quotations from the A redaction are taken from *Örvar-Odds saga* 1954. Quotations from both editions have been normalised.

associated with the legendary battle at Brávellir, said to have taken place in Norway before the settlement of Iceland, and is listed as a participant in the *Brávallaþula* and in *Sǫgubrot af fornkonungum*, as well as in Saxo's account of the battle, where he is referred to as Prince Oddi of Jæren, the location of Oddr's upbringing in the saga (Book 8). Further evidence for oral tradition informing the saga has been suggested by Lars Lönnroth in his analysis of the traditional *mannjafnaðr* exchanges during the drinking contest episode at the court of King Herrauðr (Lönnroth 1979, 94–109; see also Swenson 1991, 81–100).

Nevertheless, Jónas Kristjánsson is probably right to say that *Ǫrvar-Odds saga* 'is more like the work of an Icelandic author at his desk than the product of Norwegian oral tales' (1997, 358). This much can be seen in the saga author's learned allusions both to topographical descriptions of the far north and to the journeys of eminent Norwegians paralleling those of Oddr, as drawn from Snorri Sturluson's *Heimskringla*, Saxo, and Sturla Þórðarson's thirteenth-century *Hákonar saga Hákonarsonar* (Hermann Pálsson and Paul Edwards 1985, 282–88). These include the often turbulent dealings of Norwegian traders with Finns and Lapps, and famous treks via eastern routes to the Holy Land, such as the account in *Heimskringla* of the early twelfth-century journey undertaken by the Norwegian King Sigurðr Jórsalafari Magnússon to Jerusalem and then Syria, one which largely reflects that made by Oddr in the early redactions (Ferrari 2006, 241).[2] It is also probable that the early author knew of the northern voyages of the Norwegian trader Ohthere, as reported to King Alfred in the late ninth century and interpolated into Alfred's translation of Orosius.[3]

In addition, the saga shows certain intertextual relations with sagas of around the same period, although one cannot always be sure which saga is influencing which. The most noteworthy of these is *Norna-Gests þáttr*, whose eponymous hero, like Oddr, is cursed with long life by a malicious *vǫlva* and who, also like Oddr, receives Christian baptism. Parallels to episodes in *Ǫrvar-Odds saga* are to be found in the resentment of heathen prophecy by Ingimundr of *Vatnsdœla saga* who, like Oddr, subsequently journeys to visit his father, and, probably from the same traditions as Saxo's Arvaroddus tale, the account of the battle on Sámsey in *Hervarar saga ok*

---

[2] Ferrari also notes that the S redaction mentions Viðkunnr of Bjarkey, who in *Heimskringla*'s account of King Sigurðr's life was Sigurðr's friend, among Oddr's descendants.

[3] R. C. Boer suggested that Ohthere was the historical Oddr (1892, 102–05), a speculation that has not found favour with historians. For an edition of Ohthere's account, see Ross (1981).

Heiðreks konungs (Tolkien 1960, xii; see also Mitchell 2003, 245–56). This saga includes a version of the death-poem of Oddr's Viking blood-brother Hjálmarr, but unlike *Qrvar-Odds saga*, recounts that Hjálmarr's single combat with Angantýr is motivated by their rivalry over a woman, the Swedish princess Ingibjǫrg. It is also clear that the early author was familiar with tales of Viking adventures *í austrveg*; for example, in the S redaction, Oddr's adoption of the sobriquet *víðfǫrull* 'Wide-Traveller' at Herrauðr's court, and in all redactions concerning this episode, the names of Jólfr, a helpful peasant, and Silkisif, the king's daughter and later Oddr's wife, are particularly reminiscent of *Yngvars saga víðfǫrla*.[4]

This literary and, more important, historical embedding (bogus though this history often is) of the tale of Qrvar-Oddr is relevant to our understanding of the messages contained in the early redactions, which, as Torfi Tulinius has pointed out in his study of the *fornaldarsögur*, are set on communicating the virtue of royal governance (2002, 162). This is a message that would have had particular significance for late thirteenth- and early fourteenth-century Icelanders recently fallen under the royal jurisdiction of Norway. Associating Oddr with wide geography, antipathies to heathendom and royal personages lends to the hero a credibility and to his saga an authority that would have carried the saga audience along to an understanding of wider European politics and governance. This paper will show how the saga's concerns change over time by examining the significance of Qgmundr Eyþjófsbani, a mysterious figure in the older redactions whose role is massively expanded in the younger redactions. For the purposes of contrast and comparison, it is first necessary to consider certain key events in Oddr's life as described in the S and M redactions, which are also retained in the A redaction (see Tulinius 2002, 321–26). These are the *vǫlva*'s curse, Oddr's acceptance of Hjálmarr's Viking code, his encounter with Qgmundr, his conversion and his subsequent entry into the service of King Herrauðr.

The framing plot of *Qrvar-Odds saga* is derived from the visit of a *vǫlva* to the homestead of Oddr's foster-father, Ingjaldr, at Berurjóðr in Norway, when Oddr is yet an untested and somewhat uncooperative young man. Despite Oddr's displeasure at her presence and, even more, at her determination to predict his future, the *vǫlva* will not be put off by his threats and insults. The consequence of this confrontation is the

---

[4] Another obvious intertextual link is that between *Qrvar-Odds saga* and *Hrólfs saga Gautrekssonar*. Torfi Tulinius is probably correct in concluding that the latter is indebted to the former (2002, 168).

worse for Oddr, for she does not merely foresee his future but appears to fashion it: he will live for three hundred years, wander from land to land, win great renown but die where he started out, in Berurjóðr, from a snakebite delivered from the skull of the farm horse Faxi.[5] Although (unlike Ingjaldr) *aldri vildi Oddr blóta* 'Oddr would never make sacrifices', but instead, *trúði hann á mátt sinn ok megin* 'he trusted in his might and main' (S: *Qrvar-Odds saga* 1888, 9), there can be little doubt that Oddr fears the power of the *vǫlva*'s predictions. So much is apparent both in his violent response to her and in his efforts to confound his apparent destiny by killing and burying Faxi and determining to quit Berurjóðr for good. He may not care for heathendom but that does not mean he doubts its potency; rather, he devotes much of life to combating it. Whatever else Oddr's anti-heathendom might signify, the author of *Qrvar-Odds saga* clearly recognised that much of the entertainment value of his narrative depended on dramatising figures from a belief system that was long past having any strict congregation of adherents.[6]

After sailing to the home of his blood relatives on the northern isle of Hrafnista and receiving three magic arrows, the so-called Gusir's Gifts (*Gusisnautar*), from his father Grímr loðinkinni, Oddr ventures on a series of Viking voyages, during which he loots and desecrates a sacred mound in Permia (Bjarmaland), and establishes his ability to confound vengeful giants and overcome fierce human adversaries. Eventually he meets his match in the form of the Viking Hjálmarr and his blood-brother Þórðr, and they agree to join forces. One condition of this is that Oddr and his companions accept a *víkingalǫg* (S: *Qrvar-Odds saga* 1888, 65), a Viking code of practice. This entails a ban on eating raw flesh,[7] never robbing merchants or peasants (except, adds Hjálmarr pragmatically, to cover immediate needs), and never attacking women or forcing them aboard ship, this last injunction to be enforced on penalty of death. As was indicated on Oddr's first voyage, he is already disposed toward what might be called responsible Viking behaviour and so the pact is made. He now sails to Sweden, where, under Hjálmarr's guidance and recommendation, he receives kingly patronage for the first time.

---

[5] The prophecy and exact circumstances of Oddr's death are the same as those told about the *Rus* king Oleg in the early twelfth-century *Russian Primary Chronicle*. See Chadwick (1946, 145–74) for a fascinating discussion of the complex interrelation between *Qrvar-Odds saga* and early Russian sources.

[6] John McKinnell's discussion of *vǫlur* suggests that by the thirteenth century they were little more than literary devices and that, in wider Icelandic society, belief in their power had dwindled to folk superstition (McKinnell 2005, 95–108).

[7] S uniquely adds *ok eigi blóðdrekka*.

Further adventures follow, during which Oddr suffers the death of his foster-brother in Ireland but is compensated with a shirt of invulnerability by Princess Ǫlvǫr, whom he marries and whose kingdom he helps secure. Shortly afterwards, in much reduced circumstances, he and Hjálmarr come across the fearsomely aggressive and ugly Ǫgmundr Eyþjófsbani, who tells Oddr '*ek hefi þín leitat um hríð*' "I have been looking for you for a while" (S); an assertion which is emphasised in M with *alla mína ævi* 'all my life' (*Ǫrvar-Odds saga* 1888, 90). Neither is victorious in the ensuing sea-battle, where Ǫgmundr proves to be as impossible to harm as Oddr does, leading Oddr to suspect that his opponent is more troll than man. As a consequence of this stalemate Ǫgmundr offers a truce, which Oddr eventually accepts, only to discover later that Ǫgmundr has subsequently murdered Þórðr. Given that Þórðr was Oddr's blood-brother, Oddr is bound to seek vengeance, but Ǫgmundr is nowhere to be found. No explanation is offered as to what motivates Ǫgmundr in his search for Oddr, nor is it made clear what kind of being he is.[8] Beyond this inconclusive encounter, he never appears again in either the S or M accounts, although M alludes to a further unsuccessful search for him when Oddr leaves Sweden en route for Sámsey, and S records Oddr mentioning his encounter with him in one of the verses he composes during the drinking contest at the court of King Herrauðr.[9] From the point of view of narrative art and cohesion, Ǫgmundr is a conspicuous loose end in these early redactions.

Thereafter Oddr's good fortune seems to have deserted him, and he now suffers the loss of Hjálmarr in the ill-judged and ill-fated fight against Angantýr on Sámsey,[10] after which even more misfortune follows. It is shortly after this run of bad luck that Oddr is converted to Christianity. As Stephen Mitchell has noted, there is a marked difference between redactions S and M in their treatment of Oddr's conversion (Mitchell 1991, 109–14). According to S, Oddr goes first to Greece and from there takes ship to Sicily, where a certain Abbot Hugi comes to meet him. After receiving a sermon from Hugi on the glory of God, *lét Oddr sér þat alt vel skiljask* 'Oddr allowed himself to be convinced' (S: *Ǫrvar-Odds saga* 1888, 113). Hugi now offers to baptise Oddr but Oddr declines and *kvazk mundu sjá fyrst siðu þeira* 'said he first wanted to see their customs' (S:

---

[8] The difficulty in identifying the creature category to which Ǫgmundr belongs is considered by Ármann Jakobsson, who suggests that he might best be considered a being 'infused by sorcery' (2009, 188). This identification is made more explicit in the younger redactions.

[9] These verses are absent from M.

[10] The Sámsey episode is not present in S.

Ǫrvar-Odds saga 1888, 115). Some months later, at Hugi's request, Oddr sets out to cleanse the Greek islands of brigands. On his return to Sicily, he and all his men are baptised but Oddr, unlike his companions, soon becomes bored with the quiet life and slips away.

Perhaps the author of the M redaction detected 'the humor latent in S' (Mitchell 1991, 111), for in this account Oddr's army is shipwrecked off the coast of Aquitaine and when they come ashore and find a church building all they can do is puzzle over its significance. Oddr and his companions appear childlike in their questions about Christian beliefs and practices, although Oddr's rejoinder that their only belief is in their 'might and main' betrays something of his entrenched heroic mentality, as does his pithy remark that the Creator of all things *mun mikill vera, er þat hefir skapat* 'must be great who fashioned that' (M: *Ǫrvar-Odds saga* 1888, 114). Oddr eventually accepts the new faith but with the qualification that he *vildi sjálfr þó ráða hǫgum sínum, sem honum líkaði* 'wanted to decide his affairs himself as he liked' (M: *Ǫrvar-Odds saga* 1888, 114). In addition to this more guarded and slightly comic conversion, M adds that when Oddr tries to leave he witnesses the unprovoked killing of a bishop, whom he avenges. Despite the appreciation of the Christians and the invitation to become their leader, Oddr again discreetly exits.

Oddr now becomes a solitary wanderer, heading first to the Holy Land where he bathes in the River Jordan.[11] He then journeys into the wilderness and lives off no more than he can forage, although prior to this in S he gives royal service in Hungary (Ungaraland). Both redactions now bring Oddr into Húnaland,[12] disguised under a great cloak and calling himself *víðfǫrull* 'Wide-Traveller' in S, or dressed in bark and calling himself *næframaðr* 'Barkman' in M.[13] Having gained more magical weaponry from a peasant named Jólfr, he then presents himself before King Herrauðr, still in disguise, and declares himself to be all but talentless. Oddr is rapidly inveigled into a series of contests against the king's two champions, concluding in a declamatory drinking contest. Clearly a man

---

[11] In S he arrives in the Holy Land as the sole survivor of a shipwreck.

[12] Húnaland is difficult to locate, although it is most likely a northern kingdom in these redactions.

[13] Paul Edwards and Hermann Pálsson note that Oddr's appearance as Barkman is analogous to the folklore figure the Wild Man of the Wood and rituals associated with death and regeneration, as described in Frazer's *Golden Bough* (Edwards and Hermann Pálsson 1970, xv–xvi). A medieval analogy can also be seen in the Middle English poem *Sir Orfeo* and perhaps also in the degeneration and restoration of Nebuchadnezzar, as told in Daniel 5.

of exceptional talent, Oddr abandons his disguise, revealing himself to be splendidly attired and youthful in appearance. The great service he then performs for Herrauðr, gathering tribute from demonic pagan adversaries in the kingdom of Bjalka, leads to his being crowned Herrauðr's successor and to marriage to the king's daughter, Silkisif.[14] All that remains is for the *vǫlva*'s prophecy to be fulfilled back at Berurjóðr.

There are certain ways in which these redactions of *Ǫrvar-Odds saga* can be read as a form of *Bildungsroman*. One would be to see Oddr's career as in certain ways similar to that of Beowulf or that of the rags-to-riches folk-tale hero.[15] Thus the unpromising youth becomes the upright warrior-supreme, who undertakes royal service and eventually achieves royal authority. Along the way there is some soul-searching, signalled not only by Oddr's conversion but also by his sojourn in the wilderness and his eventual social rehabilitation. On the one hand, this would seem to be straightforward enough, yet, on the other, there is a significant ideological tension to take into account: that between the heathendom that, from the outset, determines Oddr's preternaturally long life, and his Christian credentials. Another way of reading Oddr's career, as considered by Torfi Tulinius (2002, 159–64), derives from the underlying hagiographic narrative model for his saga. The *vita*-like focus on the life of a single individual, Oddr's violent opposition to heathendom, his willing embrace of Hjálmarr's *víkingalǫg* and his acquiescence in the wisdom of Abbot Hugi are all suggestive of moral and spiritual growth. Yet this reading is also unsatisfactory for two reasons: first, as Torfi says, Oddr is evidently no saint; second, here again the paradox of a Christian hero living his life within the context of a heathen prophecy is overlooked. The question, then, is this: how much importance should we attach to Oddr's conversion?

On the face of it, Oddr's conversion in the S redaction appears somewhat perfunctory. There is no indication that he has gained any sophisticated understanding of Christian teachings, and his journey to the Holy Land is very briefly described, as it were *en passant*. After this there is no explicit mention of Christian values at any point in the saga. The M redaction is even less convincing on this matter, as the author seems to be more concerned with amusing his audience than conveying any notion

---

[14] See Lassen (2009, 256–67) for a discussion of the theological implications of Oddr's anti-paganism in this episode and elsewhere in the various redactions of his saga.

[15] This tale-type is listed in Boberg (1966) under 'L. Reversal of Fortune: L101. Unpromising hero (*male Cinderella*)'. The Norwegian folk-tale sequence 'Boots' also has certain similarities (Dasent 1888, 36–38, 48–49 and 215–21).

of Oddr finding some kind of spiritual accommodation. Lars Lönnroth's enlightening study of the concept of the 'noble heathen' does, however, seem to have some broad application to *Ǫrvar-Odds saga*, particularly in the medieval Icelandic 'need to reconcile pride in pagan ancestors and contemporary Christian belief' (1969, 4).[16] Certainly Oddr does appear to represent aspects of 'Natural Law' and 'Natural Religion' before his conversion but, beyond it, there is no deeper conviction that would indicate any revelation from the Holy Spirit. Nor is it quite the case that Oddr's conversion dramatically alters his perception of royal service, for he appears to recognise the importance of this after his service to the Swedish king with Hjálmarr, thereafter assuming the role of Commander in Chief in Ireland as husband of Princess Ǫlvǫr, and, shortly after this, helping a dispossessed Viking achieve kingship in England, all of which occurs some time before he is baptised. This being the case, Oddr's conversion may better be regarded as convention and orthodoxy; a way for the *sagnamaðr* to 'make his pagan hero, whose not so Christian exploits he has been indulgently describing, acceptable to a Christian audience' (Lönnroth 1969, 20).[17]

As much as anything, then, Oddr's conversion is a literary concession to present-day cultural values, albeit a necessary one. In keeping with his Heroic Age origins, Oddr's true belief appears to be in his *mátt ok megin*, but what is required of him is that he find an appropriate direction for it. A more profitable line of investigation, therefore, would be to consider Oddr's development in terms of the need for social order. The message of the early redactions, suggests Torfi Tulinius, is that 'one can win honour only by complying with certain rules and consenting to integration with the social structure that governs other members of that society' (Tulinius 2002, 162). Sustained upward mobility 'must come by way of court'. If royal service is the positive in the saga, the negative is all that seeks to confound or contradict it.[18] This is represented by anything associated with heathendom.

On only two occasions does Oddr fail to overcome these negatives. The first is the prophecy of the *vǫlva*, both an unwelcome intimation of mortality and an offence against nature, but evidently an ineluctable force. The second is his encounter with the enigmatic Ǫgmundr Eyþjófsbani; an

---

[16] Lönnroth does not discuss *Ǫrvar-Odds saga* in his study.

[17] In respect of the issues of honour and revenge, Lönnroth also points out the pragmatic overlap between pagan and Christian views (1969, 23–29).

[18] Alexey Eremenko sees these positives and negatives as a structural divide between the unethical 'magic world' and the ethical 'real world' (2006, 217–22).

opponent of Oddr's that is consistently denoted as non-human, and the only aggressor that he fails to overcome. Both these figures are anomalous in terms of the ideals concerning European kingship that are at the heart of the S and M redactions. Yet, while the *vǫlva*'s curse grants to the saga a satisfying symmetry, Ǫgmundr's role lacks narrative coherence. It is tempting to regard Ǫgmundr's fleeting but consequential appearance either as signifying Oddr's mortal limitations or as indicative of something unresolved in what the Marxist critic Fredric Jameson called a narrative's 'political unconscious' (Jameson 1981); in other words as symbolising a profound social tension below the level of the saga's plot formulations. Perhaps, however, this would be to rest too much on too little, and a more likely explanation, provocative though this may be, is that the peculiarity of Ǫgmundr in the early redactions is no more than an instance of poor composition. There may well have been a number of reasons why fifteenth-century redactors sought to reformulate *Ǫrvar-Odds saga*, audience taste not being the least of them, but the unrealised narrative potential of Ǫgmundr was surely something that was noticed. In seeking to rectify this problem, they effectively produced a very different saga.

The first major interpolation in the A redaction occurs immediately after Oddr's journey to the Holy Land, when he wanders alone into the wilderness. Here he is carried to the nest of a huge vulture from which he sees no escape, until a giant in a stone boat rescues him and takes him to Giantland (*Risaland*). Unlike the giants that he battled during his adventures in Permia, this one is amiable, if somewhat stupid. Oddr is given to the giant's daughter as a plaything and, much to everyone's surprise, he gets her pregnant. After advising the giant how he might win a contest to become king of Giantland, Oddr departs, having agreed that his child should be sent to him at the age of ten, should it be a boy. Restored to prosperity by a reward from the giant, now a king, Oddr encounters the mysterious Rauðgrani (Redbeard), a figure about whom the author later, rather neutrally, remarks, *Þykkir mǫnnum sem Óðinn muni þat verit hafa reyndar* 'People reckon that in fact it must have been Óðinn' (*Ǫrvar-Odds saga* 1954, 297).[19] Oddr confides to Rauðgrani his wish to take vengeance on Ǫgmundr Eyþjófsbani, whereupon he is informed that Ǫgmundr is a demonic creature specifically engineered

---

[19] Following Boer's edition, critics have concluded that Rauðgrani and Óðinn are one and the same, and that therefore the assistance accepted by Oddr from Óðinn is inconsistent with his anti-paganism (see, for example, Kroesen 1993, 744). It is, however, worth noting that the author distances himself from this certainty. For an examination of Óðinn in the *fornaldarsögur*, see Lassen 2001, 205–19.

by the Permians to kill Oddr in revenge for his desecration of their sacred sites. The otherwise puzzling statement in the M redaction that Qgmundr's search for Oddr has been lifelong is thus rationalised.

There now follow four episodes devoted to Oddr's struggle against Qgmundr, during which time Oddr kills Qgmundr's half-human, half-beast mother (a *finngálkn*), Qgmundr kills Oddr's formidable giant son, and Qgmundr marries the giantess Geirríðr, daughter of Geirrǫðr, both of whom Oddr also kills.[20] Oddr's feud against Qgmundr, interspersed with more Viking adventures in the company of new blood-brothers as arranged by Rauðgrani, takes him across the Viking world. Nothing is resolved one way or the other, although Qgmundr is facially mutilated in the last of this sequence of fights with Oddr. From this point Rauðgrani plays no further part, being, as the author tells us, disinclined to participate in violent conflict and preferring to encourage others toward this end. If this is Óðinn, he is a parody of his former mythological self.

Hereafter the A redaction follows S and M from the point where Oddr arrives in Herrauðr's kingdom (here set in Russia/Garðaríki) right through to Oddr's devastation of pagan Bjalka (said here to be in the region of Antioch) and his subsequent elevation to kingship. The final meeting with Qgmundr is then recounted. Qgmundr is calling himself Kvillánus and is ruling vast territories from his court in Novgorod (Hólmgarðr). He wears a mask, partly for cosmetic reasons. Once Oddr realises who this is, a battle ensues in which Oddr kills Qgmundr's son and Qgmundr kills the last of Oddr's blood-brothers. Come nightfall, with Novgorod and Qgmundr's army all but destroyed, Oddr slips away. One more interpolation follows in which Oddr successfully champions a certain dispossessed king against his usurper, an episode that Oddr's death-poem, his *ævidrápa*, associates with the legendary battle at Brávellir (verse 63), but which otherwise carries little narrative significance.[21] Later, settled back in his kingdom, Oddr receives costly gifts and offers of reconciliation from Qgmundr which he accepts, realising that his opponent is more *andi en maðr* 'a spirit than a man' (*Örvar-Odds saga* 1954, 337). Beyond this, the trajectory of Oddr's life is the same as that in the S and M redactions.

[20] There is a mythological reference here to Þórr's struggle against Geirröðr as given in the late tenth-century *Þórsdrápa*, attributed to Eilífr Goðrúnarson, and in Snorri Sturluson's *Skáldskaparmál* (for both see Faulkes, ed., 1998, I 24–30; and Faulkes, trans., 1987, 81–86).

[21] Structurally, this episode resembles one that is otherwise unique to the S redaction and takes place between Oddr's visit to the Holy Land and his arrival in Herrauðr's kingdom.

The world of Ǫrvar-Oddr in the younger redactions is much more emphatically two worlds. There is still the 'real' world of the older redactions, predominantly a materialistic place where Oddr seeks to improve himself and ultimately his society, but where there is the vexation of contrary forces from an old order that occasionally precipitates slippage into unwelcome strangeness. Although the hero has the mettle, the equipment and the predisposition to combat these forces, they nonetheless haunt him and finally, in the curse laid upon him, encompass his life. But in the otherworld of the younger redactions, these same forces are multiplied and preoccupy the hero to no lasting advantage. How, then, might this expanded fantastical world, and particularly the figure of Ǫgmundr Eyþjófsbani, be understood in a fifteenth-century context and more generally in terms of medieval Icelandic literary traditions?

One approach to understanding Ǫgmundr's symbolic function is indicated by Paul Edwards and Hermann Pálsson, who tentatively suggest that there are sufficient similarities between Oddr and Ǫgmundr to regard the latter as 'an extension of Odd's own self' and 'a perspective of Odd as his enemies might see him' (1970, xvii–xviii). Ǫgmundr, following this line, would be what Derek Brewer in other connections refers to as a symbolic 'split' of the protagonist (Brewer, 1980). This psychoanalytical approach is rejected by Fulvio Ferrari on the grounds that it 'assumes a point of view which is a little bit too modern' (2006, 246).[22] Nevertheless, there can be no doubt that a fifteenth-century saga audience was quite familiar with ideas presenting human experience, both outer and inner, in terms of opposites, not least from fundamental Christian dualisms. Similarly, the concept of a troubled psychology had been projected as narrative characters in Old Icelandic literature since the time of the *Íslendingasögur*; for example, one only need think of the dream women that trouble the outlawed hero of *Gísla saga Súrssonar*. Reading Ǫgmundr as Oddr's 'dark side' entails seeing a fracture in the hero's apprehension of his own reality, which is framed in the saga as a sub-mythic realisation of the conflict between chaos and order or past and present. In ideological terms, this conflict may suggest that between progressive Christian modernity and regressive heathen tradition, but as both of these forces are aspects of the same cultural equation they are, in effect, conditions of each other. Accordingly, Oddr and Ǫgmundr are mutually indispensable as they are the self-same thing.

---

[22] Ferrari argues that Ǫgmundr's role 'contributes to taking from Oddr part of his greatness' and that the author's purpose was 'to compose an interesting and exciting story' which would be 'more adequate to the taste of a refined and learned audience' (2006, 246).

Torfi Tulinius takes a more historicist approach, by which he identifies Ǫgmundr as a figure of death (2002, 163–64). This is intriguing on two counts. First, as Torfi observes, a preoccupation with death was intensified across Europe during the fourteenth and fifteenth centuries as a result of the Black Death. The plague caused the loss of between one and two thirds of the population of Iceland in 1402–04, and had had drastic effects on the Icelandic economy since the mid-fourteenth century, owing to its impact on Norway (Vahtola 2003, 567). Second, such an interpretation of Ǫgmundr's symbolic significance is consistent with Oddr's inevitable mortal obsessions. Ǫgmundr-as-death explains why Oddr cannot kill him, and may even suggest a 'death wish that Oddr exhibits by his zealous pursuit' (Tulinius 2002, 163). Further support for this theory has been suggested by Ármann Jakobsson, who notes in the description of Ǫgmundr's 'manufacture' by the Permians, as recounted by Rauðgrani (see *Ǫrvar-Odds saga* 1954, 279–83), and in assessments of his creature category given elsewhere in the saga, that there is the possibility that he is already dead, an *aptrganga*.[23] This would also explain why Oddr finally recognises that Ǫgmundr is *ósigranligr* 'one who cannot be overcome' (*Ǫrvar-Odds saga* 1954, 337).

Yet a precise identification of Ǫgmundr with death, as it is personified in much other medieval art and literature, raises certain problems. Whilst Oddr is consistently frustrated in his desire to wreak vengeance on Ǫgmundr, the question remains why Ǫgmundr cannot kill Oddr, a limitation which Ǫgmundr acknowledges on more than one occasion. One would have to accept the proposition that death is constrained by the greater power of the *vǫlva*'s curse. Moreover, Ǫgmundr twice implies that Oddr could indeed bring about his death: '*En ef vit berjumsk til þrautar, þá mun ek falla fyrir þér*' "But if we fight to the end, then I will fall before you" (*Ǫrvar-Odds saga* 1954, 249); and '*En engan mann hræðumsk ek í verǫldinni nema þik, ok af þér mun ek nǫkkut illt hljóta, hvárt þat verðr fyrr eða síðar*' "But no man in the world do I fear other than you, and through you I shall suffer ill fortune, whether that be sooner or later" (*Ǫrvar-Odds saga* 1954, 292). Even though there are, then, certain contradictions in the saga regarding Ǫgmundr's nature and capacities, the fact remains that in the end neither Ǫgmundr nor Oddr succeeds in killing the other. Rather than attempting to equate Ǫgmundr with death, it might therefore be better to see Ǫgmundr as a constant reminder of Oddr's fate, a disquieting *memento mori* which will not in itself be Oddr's nemesis but against which struggle

---

[23] I am grateful to Ármann for this suggestion, which was made in personal correspondence.

is equally futile and which is, in this sense, a personification of the *vǫlva*'s curse. Thus, when Oddr says to Ǫgmundr in their final encounter, '*við þik sættumsk ek aldri*' "I shall never come to terms with you" (*Örvar-Odds saga* 1954, 335), he is speaking of an age-old resentment. Notably, it is shortly after Oddr's eventual reconciliation with Ǫgmundr, which by this reading would signify an acceptance of his fate, that he disregards his own vow never to return to Berurjóðr and heads north, there to meet his end.

The vastly increased prominence of Ǫgmundr in the younger redactions has the effect of further diminishing the significance of Oddr's conversion beyond the light treatment that is given to it in the M redaction, a treatment which the younger redactions all follow. This is not to say that these younger redactions are in some way more secularised; rather, as Oskar Bandle suggests, one might conclude that the additional Ǫgmundr material has the effect of throwing Oddr's noble character into even sharper relief, thus emphasising a Christian and chivalric perspective on the old heroic life (Bandle 1990, 62).[24] Oddr's conversion is simply a given in respect of one who stands on the front line against the demonic and the irrational. Much the same can be said about the implicit message in the older redactions concerning the societal value of monarchical authority, something which by the fifteenth century would, in any case, have been a far less controversial issue; indeed, also a given. Here, Oddr's rise to kingship has more the look of a will to power, the remarkable accomplishment of a talented yet troubled individual. It is this troubled element that is central to the account of Oddr's life in the A redaction. Although Ǫgmundr may be interpreted as an aspect of Oddr's psychology, his inner landscape, or as a personification of Oddr's curse in his outer landscape, the issue that is raised is one that concerns identity. This matter of identity, whether considered in terms of Oddr's character or in terms of a fifteenth-century Icelandic cultural formulation, has significant bearing on our understanding of the younger redactions, particularly as regards the saga's literary relations.

The fifteenth-century A and B texts are preceded in their manuscripts by the short sagas of Oddr's ancestors; respectively, *Ketils saga hængs*, the tale of Oddr's grandfather, and *Gríms saga loðinkinna*, that of his father.[25] R. C. Boer identified a number of motifs common to these sagas

---

[24] One may, however, wonder how Oddr's copulation with a giantess shortly after his conversion might have been regarded by a Christian audience, especially as this union is described without censure.

[25] A third saga concerning the Hrafnistumenn preserved in the same fifteenth-century manuscript group as A is *Áns saga bogsveigis*. The hero, Án, is the great-grandson of Ketill Hæng and Sigríðr.

and *Ǫrvar-Odds saga* (Boer 1892, 97–100), and there have been several studies analysing elements of the 'Bear's Son' folktale-type apparent in them (for example, Jorgensen 1975, 91–95, and Pizarro 1976–77, 263–81). The author of the S redaction certainly knew the traditions associated with these heroes of Hrafnista, as is clear from the reference he makes to Oddr's lineage at the outset of the saga, including Oddr's great-grandfather Hallbjǫrn Hálftroll.[26] Given that the likely provenance of *Ketils saga hængs* is thirteenth-century (Ciklamini 1993, 353; Tulinius 2007, 452), perhaps somewhat older than *Gríms saga loðinkinna*, it is quite feasible that he was familiar with it, but the extent to which he was influenced by the saga is questionable; for example, when Grímr gives Oddr the magic arrows, he says, '*þær vann ek af Gusi Finnakonungi*' "I won these from Gusir, king of the Finns" (S: *Ǫrvar-Odds saga* 1888, 25). This is not consistent with either of the two ancestor sagas, where it is Ketill who wins the arrows, Grímr only inheriting them. The origin of the magic arrows is brought into line with the ancestor sagas in the slightly younger M redaction and in all subsequent redactions.

Perhaps, then, the authors of S and M knew the sagas of Ketill and Grímr, and perhaps also the author of M sought to correlate his redaction with them, but there is little sign of either redactors exploring the themes of these sagas, except in so far as Oddr, like his Hrafnistumenn forebears, has encounters with non-human otherness. Unlike both Ketill and Grímr, however, Oddr's dealing with otherworldly beings in the early redactions is fairly straightforward: he simply kills them, or tries to. This, as we know, is not quite the case in the A redaction, where it is reasonable to assume that the author was perfectly familiar with the *Ǫrvar-Odds saga* prequels.

Much of the drama of *Ketils saga hængs* arises from the conflict between Ketill and his father Hallbjǫrn. While Ketill has an adventurous spirit, his father is determined to keep him on a short leash, primarily in an attempt to shield him from the mysterious and dangerous world of non-humans that exists beyond the safe confines of the farm. Hallbjǫrn's anxieties would seem to stem from his own deep familiarity with this world, for he is a half-troll. But Ketill will not be restrained, and persists in venturing further and further north where he has a series of encounters with alien and savage creatures, leading eventually to his winning Gusir's Gifts. Yet not all those he meets threaten him; he befriends the Lapp Brúni and, at Brúni's invitation, he couples with his unprepossessing daughter, Hrafnhildr, the result of which is the birth of Grímr. As Hallbjǫrn considers Hrafnhildr to

---

[26] Hallbjǫrn is not mentioned in the genealogy given in M.

be a troll, she is banned from the farm, and he subsequently forces Ketill to marry Sigríðr, a local girl by whom Ketill has a daughter. Ketill raises Grímr in the full knowledge of trolldom and takes the enlightened view that his daughter should not be married against her will, a view that forces him to fight a number of duels until a satisfactory match can be made.

The much shorter *Gríms saga loðinkinna* is a variant of the frog-prince tale, wherein the gender roles are reversed. Grímr's fiancée, Lofthæna, has the misfortune to have a trollish stepmother, who has her abducted and transmogrified. In his search for her, Grímr has numerous fights against trolls and berserks, until he shares a bed with a helpful but hideous troll-woman who, when he wakes, turns out to be Lofthæna, now restored to human form. They marry and Lofthæna bears Grímr a daughter, whom, just as was the case with Ketill and his daughter, he has to protect from aggressive suitors, in this case a roughneck in the company of twelve berserks. Grímr's second in the ensuing duel is Ingjaldr of Berurjóðr, who in *Ǫrvar-Odds saga* is foster-father to Grímr's son, Oddr.

The world of the Hrafnistumenn in the ancestor sagas is almost entirely fantastical. There is no safe harbour with kings, no sanctuary among Christian communities, no companionship of Viking comrades, no career ladder of human strife to climb. While the farmstead appears to function as a metonym for human society, it is troubled from within, for the heroes are drawn beyond its limits toward a place of magically endowed chaos. But this is a place where they somehow belong. One problem for Ketill and Grímr is that they have troll blood running through them, making their relations with non-humans, most frequently denoted as trolls, somewhat equivocal (Arnold 2005, 134–38). The signification of the creature-category 'troll' in these sagas is quite elastic and can include genuine monsters as well as Lapps and Finns, and it is therefore best to understand the meaning of troll as 'something that is strange and peculiar, exceeding normality in some way' (Ármann Jakobsson 2008, 46). Abnormality, however, defines the heroes almost as much as it does their otherworldly adversaries and associates. Hallbjǫrn tries to breed out this abnormality but fails when the errant Ketill succeeds in exaggerating it in Hallbjǫrn's grandson, Grímr. This commingling of normal and abnormal blood is what Oddr inherits, in almost exactly the same measure as his grandfather Ketill.

In *Ketils saga hængs* the 'normality versus abnormality' theme is first articulated as a conflict between Hallbjǫrn's social ideals and a past, in part designated as Hallbjǫrn's past, that exercises a peculiar hold over Ketill. Whereas in the older redactions of *Ǫrvar-Odds saga* the hero strives to repudiate all that represents the past, in the younger redactions, as in the ancestor sagas, past and present are intertwined. So it is that Oddr, like his ancestors, has ambivalent relations with the denizens of the otherworld. He is fully prepared to fight and kill those that threaten or offend him, but is equally prepared to accept help and comfort from those that do not, as is apparent when he takes guidance from Rauðgrani and when he sires a giant son. If the fantastical world of *Ǫrvar-Odds saga* is understood to represent the pre-Christian world of the Eddas, and Oddr as representing a relationship with this ancient legacy, then the mutual enmity and final reconciliation between him and Ǫgmundr Eyþjófsbani suggests a cultural ambivalence rooted in a contemporary apprehension of a historical identity. As Mitchell has noted in respect of *Ketils saga hængs* particularly and the *fornaldarsögur* generally, 'writers, consumers, and so on were also participating in the "salvage ethnography" of a "memory culture" [which] was likely to have been of a recalled, idealized, and generally bygone world' (2009, 292–93; see also Mitchell 1991, 134–36). Inevitably, this is a contradictory condition in *Ǫrvar-Odds saga*, for while Oddr's efforts are often targeted against this past, it is a past that ultimately defines him.

Like the psychoanalytical or historicist reading of the problematic connection between Oddr and Ǫgmundr in the A redaction, this reading of it, one signifying a complex interconnectedness between past and present at a subtextual level, will also not allow them to be understood outside their mutual animosity. Oddr and Ǫgmundr are two sides of the same coin, whose opposition is, paradoxically, an expression of their unity. Although it may be to assume too much intention on the part of the fifteenth-century redactors, it is not unlikely that their knowledge of the sagas of Oddr's ancestors led them to amplify the fantastical elements, most specifically through the role of Ǫgmundr, thus producing a satisfactory explanation for Ǫgmundr's antipathies, which in the early redactions are inexplicable. Through this amplification the newly formed saga complicates the more straightforward diametric oppositions between a heathen past and Christian Europe, as set out in the early redactions. An obvious cultural analogy to this lies in the question what it might mean to have inherited an extraordinary mythological and legendary store which in many ways gave unique definition to medieval Icelandic identity, but which ill befitted the ideological values of the present. In these later accounts of the hero, however, there is some sense of an accommodation having been reached: Oddr and Ǫgmundr will co-exist. Perhaps, then, the claims of the past are somehow being validated, for if Oddr not only signifies a relationship with this past but also signifies the brilliance of it, then its claims on him, as symbolised in the *vǫlva*'s curse, could also be interpreted as those of the old heroic world on the medieval present.

In conclusion, the meaning of Ǫgmundr Eyþjófsbani in the S and M redactions can only be discerned in his apparent lack of meaning as a character that is singularly badly integrated into an otherwise conservative narrative which primarily functions to advertise the benefits of monarchy. Despite this, as Ǫgmundr is the only one of Oddr's enemies that escapes his vengeance; he has a unique association with the *vǫlva*'s curse, that other offence that Oddr cannot cancel out. In the A redaction, where Ǫgmundr is given a starring role as the protagonist's chief adversary, this association is emphatic. While the revised saga could well be seen as broken-backed as a result of the interpolations—an awkward merging of a tale conveying a particular thirteenth- and fourteenth-century political ideal with a fifteenth-century taste for romance fantasy—so powerful is the effect of expanding Ǫgmundr's role that the impact of his presence is second only to that of Oddr. Unlike the caricature of ancient wisdom given by the Rauðgrani/Óðinn figure or the burlesque adventures that Oddr is given among the giants, an episode which appears to parody Ketill hængr's dalliance with Brúni and Hrafnhildr the Lapp, Ǫgmundr is a serious problem for the hero. Whether one views him as a product of fifteenth-century morbid anxieties or as indicative of an unconscious formulation concerning cultural values or, indeed, both, Ǫgmundr Eyþjófsbani in the younger redactions is Oddr's curse reified. Thus, in their reformulation of *Ǫrvar-Odds saga* along the same thematic lines as the ancestor sagas, the younger redactors delivered a tale in which the *vǫlva*'s curse is signified throughout. As a result, the saga's latent meaning or 'political unconscious' suggests a conceptualisation of cultural dynamics that is more sophisticated and perhaps more assured, more 'to terms', than that of the strictly dichotomised world of the older redactions.

APPENDIX

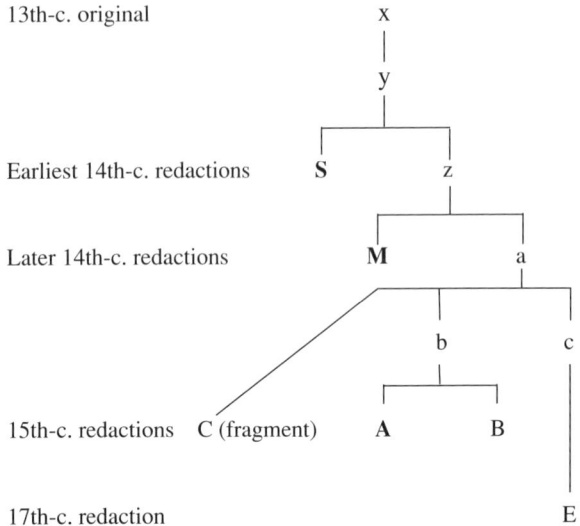

Manuscript stemma after R. C. Boer (*Qrvar-Odds saga* 1888, xxxiv). Mss deduced are assigned in lower case. Mss considered in this study are marked in bold.

Bibliography

Áns saga bogsveigis. In *Fornaldarsögur norðurlanda* 1954 I–IV. Ed. Guðni Jónsson, II 365–403.
Ármann Jakobsson 2008. 'The Trollish Acts of Þorgrímr the Witch: The Meanings of *troll* and *ergi* in Medieval Iceland'. *Saga-Book* XXXII, 39–68.
Ármann Jakobsson 2009. 'Identifying the Ogre: The Legendary Sagas'. In *Fornaldarsagaerne, myter og virkelighed*. Ed. Agneta Ney et al., 181–200.
Arnold, Martin 2005. '*Hvat er tröll nema þat?*: The Cultural History of the Troll'. In *The Shadow-Walkers. Jacob Grimm's Mythology of the Monstrous*. Ed. Tom Shippey, 111–55.
Bandle, Oskar 1990. 'Um Þróun *Örvar-Odds sögu*'. *Gripla* 7, 51–71.
Boberg, Inger M. 1966. *Motif-Index of Early Icelandic Literature*.
Boer, R. C. 1892. 'Über die *Qrvar-Odds saga*'. *Arkiv för nordisk filologi* 8, 97–139.
Brewer, Derek 1980. *Symbolic Stories: Traditional Narratives of the Family Drama in English Literature*.
Chadwick, N. K. 1946. *The Beginnings of Russian History: An Enquiry into Sources*.
Ciklamini, Marlene 1993. '*Ketils saga hængs*'. In *Medieval Scandinavia. An Encyclopedia*. Ed. Phillip Pulsiano, 352–53.
Dasent, Sir George Webbe, trans., 1888. *Popular Tales from the Norse*.

Edwards, Paul and Hermann Pálsson, trans., 1970. *Arrow-Odd: A Medieval Novel*.
Ellis Davidson, Hilda, ed., and Peter Fisher, trans., 1979–80. *Saxo Grammaticus. The History of the Danes, Books I–IX*.
Eremenko, Alexey 2006. 'The Dual World of the *Fornaldarsögur*'. In *The Fantastic in Old Norse/Icelandic Literature: Sagas and the British Isles. Preprint Papers of the Thirteenth International Saga Conference, Durham and York 6th–12th August 2006*, vol. 1. Ed. John McKinnell et al., 217–22.
Faulkes, Anthony, ed., 1982. Snorri Sturluson, *Edda: Prologue and Gylfaginning*.
Faulkes, Anthony, trans., 1987. Snorri Sturluson, *Edda*.
Faulkes, Anthony, ed., 1998. Snorri Sturluson, *Edda: Skáldskaparmál*.
Ferrari, Fulvio 2006. 'Gods, Warlocks and Monsters in the *Örvar-Odds saga*'. In *The Fantastic in Old Norse/Icelandic Literature: Sagas and the British Isles. Preprint Papers of the Thirteenth International Saga Conference, Durham and York 6th–12th August 2006*, vol. 1. Ed. John McKinnell et al., 241–47.
Gísla saga Súrssonar. In *Vestfirðinga sǫgur* 1943. Ed. Björn K. Þórólfsson and Guðni Jónsson. Íslenzk fornrit VI.
Gríms saga loðinkinna 1954. In *Fornaldarsögur norðurlanda* 1954 I–IV. Ed. Guðni Jónsson, II 183–98.
Heimskringla 1941–51. Ed. Bjarni Aðalbjarnarson. Íslenzk fornrit XXVI–XXVIII.
Hermann Pálsson and Paul Edwards, trans., 1985. *Seven Viking Romances*.
Jameson, Fredric 1981. *The Political Unconscious: Narrative as a Socially Symbolic Act*.
Jónas Kristjánssson 1997. *Eddas and Sagas. Iceland's Medieval Literature*. Trans. Peter Foote.
Jorgensen, Peter A. 2000. 'The Two-Troll Variant of the Bear's Son Folktale in *Hálfdanar saga Brönufóstra* and *Gríms saga loðinkinna*'. *Arv* 31, 35–43.
Ketils saga hængs 1954. In *Fornaldarsögur norðurlanda* 1954 I–IV. Ed. Guðni Jónsson, II 149–81.
Kroesen, Riti 1993. '*Ǫrvar-Odds saga*'. In *Medieval Scandinavia. An Encyclopedia*. Ed. Phillip Pulsiano et al., 744.
Lassen, Annette 2003. 'Den prosaiske Odin. Fortidssagaerne som mytografi'. In *Fornaldarsagornas struktur och ideologi. Handlingar från ett symposium i Uppsala 31.8–2.9 2001*. Ed. Ármann Jakobsson et al., 205–19.
Lassen, Annette 2009. 'Skurðgoð, trégoð, hofgyðjur og heiðinglig hof: En gruppe hedenske elementer og deres kontekst i *Ǫrvar-Odds saga*, *Sturlaugs saga starfsama* og *Bósa saga*'. In *Fornaldarsagaerne, myter og virkelighed*. Ed. Agneta Ney et al., 255–79.
Lönnroth, Lars 1969. 'The Noble Heathen: A Theme in the Sagas'. *Scandinavian Studies* 41, 1–29.
Lönnroth, Lars 1979. 'The double scene of Arrow-Odd's drinking contest'. In *Medieval Narrative: A Symposium*. Ed. Hans Bekker-Nielsen et al., 94–119.
McKinnell, John 2005. *Meeting the Other in Norse Myth and Legend*.
Mitchell, Stephen A. 1991. *Heroic Sagas and Ballads*.
Mitchell, Stephen 2003. 'The *fornaldarsögur* and Nordic Balladry: The Sámsey Episode across Genres'. In *Fornaldarsagornas struktur och ideologi*.

Handlingar från ett symposium i Uppsala 31.8–2.9 2001. Ed. Ármann Jakobsson et al., 245–56.
Mitchell, Stephen A. 2009. 'The Supernatural and the *fornaldarsögur*. The Case of *Ketils saga hængs*'. In *Fornaldarsagaerne, myter og virkelighed*. Ed. Agneta Ney et al., 281–91.
Norna-Gests þáttr. In *Fornaldarsögur norðurlanda* 1954 I–IV. Ed. Guðni Jónsson, I 305–35.
Pizarro, Joaquín Martínez 1976–77. 'Transformations of the Bear's Son Tale in the Sagas of the Hrafnistumenn'. *Arv* 32–33, 263–81.
Ross, Alan S. C. 1981. *The Terfinnas and Beormas of Ohthere*.
Swenson, Karen 1991. *Performing Definitions: Two Genres of Insult in Old Norse Literature*.
Tolkien, Christopher, ed. and trans., 1960. *The Saga of King Heidrek the Wise*.
Torfi H. Tulinius 2002. *The Matter of the North: The Rise of Literary Fiction in Thirteenth-Century Iceland*. Trans. Randi C. Eldevik.
Torfi H. Tulinius, 2005. 'Sagas of Icelandic Prehistory (*fornaldarsögur*)'. In *A Companion to Old Norse-Icelandic Literature and Culture*. Ed. Rory McTurk, 447–61.
Vahtola, Jouko 2003. 'Population and Settlement'. In *The Cambridge History of Scandinavia*. Volume 1: *Prehistory to 1520*. Ed. Knut Helle, 559–80.
Vatnsdœla saga 1939. Ed. Einar Ól. Sveinsson. Íslenzk fornrit VIII.
Yngvars saga víðförla. In *Fornaldarsögur norðurlanda* 1954 I–IV. Ed. Guðni Jónsson, II 423–59.
Ǫrvar-Odds saga 1888. Ed. R. C. Boer.
Ǫrvar-Odds saga 1954. In *Fornaldarsögur norðurlanda* 1954 I–IV. Ed. Guðni Jónsson, II 199–363.

THE TALE OF HOGNI AND HEDINN

TRANSLATED BY WILLIAM MORRIS AND EIRÍKR MAGNÚSSON

Introduction

By CARL PHELPSTEAD

The first Icelandic saga to be translated into English in its entirety was a *fornaldarsaga*. George Stephens's 1839 translation of *Friðþiófs saga hins frækna* was the first of three versions of that saga published in the nineteenth century. Though rarely read in the twentieth century or today, the saga was popular with, and highly praised by, Victorian readers (if not as popular as the 1824 poetic reworking of the saga by a Swedish bishop, Esias Tegnér, which was translated into English at least fifteen times before 1914; see Wawn 1994; 2000a, ch. 5). The second English translation of *Friðþjófs saga* was published by William Morris and Eiríkr Magnússon in 1871 (and republished in their *Three Northern Love Stories* in 1875). The many saga translations by Morris and his Icelandic collaborator exerted a seminal influence on Victorian and later enthusiasm for the Vikings: one recent commentator claims that 'probably no serious saga translator since 1869 has been totally uninfluenced' by their work (Kennedy 2007, 54), though one must acknowledge that such influence has often taken the form of a reaction against their stylistic preferences.

William Morris (1834–96) is now better known for his design and craft work than for his writings, but he was a prolific and popular poet, translator, prose romance-writer and political commentator. His earliest published writings evince knowledge of, and enthusiastic interest in, Norse and Scandinavian material, and this became a dominant interest when he began to learn to read Icelandic, and to translate from the language into English, in collaboration with the Icelandic scholar Eiríkr Magnússon (1833–1913), resident in England, whom Morris met in 1868.[1] In just a few years the two men made a remarkable number of translations of Icelandic sagas: most were produced between 1868 and the early 1870s, though some were not published until twenty years later as part of what became a six-volume collection, *The Saga Library* (1891–1905).

---

[1] Eiríkr describes their meeting and collaboration in Morris 1910–15, VIII xv–xix and in Morris and Eiríkr Magnússon 1891–1905, VI vii–xvi. There is a brief account of Eiríkr's scholarly career in Aho 1996, x–xii; see also Wawn 2000b.

Besides translating many *Íslendingasögur*, the whole of *Heimskringla* and *Friðþjófs saga*, Morris and Eiríkr Magnússon introduced two *fornaldarsögur* to English readers for the first time. Their translation of *Vǫlsunga saga*—described by Morris as 'the best tale pity ever wrought' (1870, xx)—was published in 1870 together with English versions of thirteen related Eddic poems.[2] A short *fornaldarsaga* now usually known as *Sǫrla þáttr*, but called *The Tale of Hogni and Hedinn* by Morris and Eiríkr (translating its alternative title, *Héðins saga ok Hǫgna*), was published in *Three Northern Love Stories and Other Tales* in 1875; the volume also included reprints of their earlier translations of *Gunnlaugs saga* and *Friðþjófs saga*, a translation of *Víglundar saga* and a selection of shorter narratives. *The Tale of Hogni and Hedinn* is reprinted below in recognition of the importance of the work of Morris and Eiríkr Magnússon in making *fornaldarsögur* accessible to the English-speaking world.

As the reader quickly realises, Morris and Eiríkr Magnússon adopt a distinctive style for their translations from Old Icelandic, one that has evoked strongly critical reactions from many readers, and admiringly positive responses from a rather smaller number. Their approach has often been misleadingly described simply as archaism, but although they certainly use archaic vocabulary and morphological forms, this is an inadequate description. In a chapter discussing the policy decisions facing a translator from Old Icelandic, John Kennedy draws an apposite distinction between archaism and 'Icelandicised' translation, offering the translations of Morris and Eiríkr Magnússon as the best known examples of the latter approach and rightly noting that their strategy has frequently been misunderstood (Kennedy 2007, 29–36). Archaic language, both vocabulary and notably also the second person pronoun *thou* and its associated verb forms, was used by several Victorian saga translators in order to distance readers from the present and heighten their awareness of the medieval origin of the translated text. 'Icelandicising' translation, on the other hand, uses archaic words, forms and structures specifically to highlight historical connections between the English and Icelandic languages. In the present text, for example, the translators use the archaic English noun 'carl' (meaning 'man') not simply because it is archaic, but also because it recalls the Icelandic term *karl*. Their use of 'dragon' to refer to a Viking ship translates literally the Old Norse term *dreki*, whereas 'dragon-headed ship' or even 'dragon-ship' might have been more transparent to the uninitiated reader. As J. N. Swannell (1961, 377) suggests, the result of their

---

[2] The legend of the Volsungs also inspired one of Morris's major reworkings of Norse material, his long narrative poem *Sigurd the Volsung*: see Ashurst 2007.

approach is, ironically, that the saga translations of William Morris and Eiríkr Magnússon can best be appreciated by those readers whose own knowledge of Old Icelandic (and, one might add, of the history of English) enables them to appreciate the linguistic connections to which the translators draw attention by their stylistic choices: a class of reader with little need for a translation in the first place. Readers lacking such knowledge who are not disconcerted by the unfamiliar diction and sentence structure may, however, find that they too are able to appreciate the peculiar vigour achieved by Morris and his collaborator. They are particularly successful in the near-impossible task of translating skaldic verse (of which just one example occurs in *The Tale of Hogni and Hedinn*): their idiosyncratic diction seems peculiarly suited to rendering skaldic artifice.

The Tale of Hogni and Hedinn (*Sǫrla þáttr*) is a short text preserved in only one medieval manuscript: the late fourteenth-century Flateyjarbók. The tale is one of many *þættir* incorporated into the manuscript's account of the life of King Óláfr Tryggvason of Norway. It was included in C. C. Rafn's genre-defining edition of the *fornaldarsögur* (1829–30, I 389–407) and in Guðni Jónsson's popular edition of the corpus (1954, I 365–82). Besides Rafn's edition, Morris and Eiríkr Magnússon would have been able to use the edition of Flateyjarbók by Guðbrandur Vigfússon and C. R. Unger (1860–68, I 275–83). The tale begins with a mythological introduction in which Freyja obtains and then loses a necklace (perhaps the famous Brísingamen, though it is not so named in the tale); she is told that to recover it she must provoke a battle between kings which will continue for ever unless interrupted by a powerful king's Christian retainer. The focus then shifts to the Baltic exploits of Sǫrli sterki Erlingsson (hero of another *fornaldarsaga*, *Sǫrla saga sterka*). Sǫrli kills the father of Hǫgni, whom Freyja (assuming the name Gǫndul) then sets at odds with another king, Héðinn. The resulting *Hjaðningavíg* 'Battle of the followers of Héðinn' is magically prolonged for 143 years until finally brought to an end by Ívarr ljómi, retainer of the Christian king Óláfr Tryggvason.

The mythological opening section unusually portrays Freyja and Loki as courtly retainers of Óðinn. Freyja's sexual relationship with Óðinn is unexpected, but compatible with allusions to her sexual appetite in other texts; Loki's transformations in the tale are likewise not recorded elsewhere but are comparable with those he undergoes in other sources. The *þáttr* is of particular interest to Anglophone readers because of the reference to the Brosings' necklace (*Brosinga mene*) in the Old English *Beowulf* (l.1199; see Damico 1983) and the appearance of names associated with the *Hjaðningavíg* legend in the poems *Widsith* and *Deor*. The story of the *Hjaðningavíg* is also recounted or alluded to in several other medieval texts, including Bragi Boddason's *Ragnarsdrápa* (sts 8–12), Snorri Sturluson's *Skáldskaparmál* (as noted by Morris and Eiríkr Magnússon (1875, 3; they translate the relevant passage: 159–60)) and Saxo Grammaticus's *Gesta Danorum* (see Rowe 2002 on the connections of the *þáttr* with other texts).

Bibliography and Suggested Further Reading

Aho, Gary 1996. 'Introduction'. In William Morris. *Three Northern Love Stories and Other Tales*, v–xxxvii.

Ashurst, David 2007. 'William Morris and the Volsungs'. In *Old Norse Made New: Essays on the Post-Medieval Reception of Old Norse Literature and Culture*. Ed. David Clark and Carl Phelpstead, 43–61.

Damico, Helen 1983. '*Sörlaþáttr* and the Hama Episode in *Beowulf*'. *Scandinavian Studies* 55/3, 222–35.

Driscoll, M. J., and Silvia Hufnagel. *Fornaldarsögur norðurlanda: A bibliography of manuscripts, editions, translations and secondary literature* <http://www.staff.hum.ku.dk/mjd/fornaldarsagas/> [consulted 18 January 2010]

Guðbrandur Vigfússon and C. R. Unger, eds, 1860–68. *Flateyjarbok: En Samling af norske Konge-Sagaer med indskudte mindre Fortællinger om Begivenheder i og undenfor Norge samt Annaler*.

Guðni Jónsson, ed., 1954. *Fornaldarsögur norðurlanda* I–IV.

Kennedy, John 2007. *Translating the Sagas: Two Hundred Years of Challenge and Response*.

MacCarthy, Fiona 1994. *William Morris: A Life for our Time*.

Morris, William 1910–15. *The Collected Works of William Morris*. Ed. May Morris. 24 vols.

Morris, William, and Eiríkr Magnússon, trans, 1870. *The Story of the Volsungs and Niblungs, with Certain Songs from the Elder Edda*.

Morris, William, and Eiríkr Magnússon, trans, 1875. *Three Northern Love Stories*.

Morris, William, and Eiríkr Magnússon, trans, 1891–1905. *The Saga Library*. 6 vols.

Rafn, C. C., ed., 1829–30. *Fornaldar sögur nordrlanda*.

Rowe, Elizabeth Ashman 2002. '*Sǫrla þáttr*: The Literary Adaptation of Myth and Legend'. *Saga-Book* XXVI, 38–66.

Stephens, George 1839. *Frithiof's Saga: A Legend of Norway*.

Swannell, J. N. 1961. 'William Morris as an Interpreter of Old Norse'. *Saga-Book* XV, 365–82.

Wawn, Andrew 1994. 'The Cult of "Stalwart Frith-thjof" in Victorian Britain'. In *Northern Antiquity: The Post-Medieval Reception of Edda and Saga*. Ed. Andrew Wawn, 211–54.

Wawn, Andrew 2000a. *The Vikings and the Victorians: Inventing the Old North in Nineteenth-century Britain*.

Wawn, Andrew 2000b. *'Fast er drukkið og fátt lært': Eiríkur Magnússon, Old Northern Philology, and Victorian Cambridge*. H. M. Chadwick Memorial Lectures 11.

The Tale of Hogni and Hedinn

Chapter I. Of Freyja and the Dwarfs

East of Vanaquisl in Asia was the land called Asialand or Asiahome, but the folk that dwelt there was called Æsir, and their chief town was Asgard. Odin was the name of the king thereof, and therein was a right holy place of sacrifice. Niord and Frey Odin made Temple-priests thereover; but the daughter of Niord was Freyia, and she was fellow to Odin and his concubine.

Now there were certain men in Asia, whereof one was called Alfrigg, the second Dwalin, the third Berling, the fourth Grerr: these had their abode but a little space from the King's hall, and were men so wise in craftsmanship, that they laid skilful hand on all matters; and such-like men as they were did men call dwarfs. In a rock was their dwelling, and in that day they mingled more with menfolk than as now they do.

Odin loved Freyia full sore, and withal she was the fairest woman of that day: she had a bower that was both fair and strong; insomuch, say men, that if the door were shut to, none might come into the bower aforesaid without the will of Freyia.

Now on a day went Freyia afoot by that rock of the dwarfs, and it lay open: therein were the dwarfs a-smithying a golden collar, and the work was at point to be done: fair seemed that collar to Freyia, and fair seemed Freyia to the dwarfs.

Now would Freyia buy the collar of them, and bade them in return for it silver and gold, and other good things. They said they lacked not money, yet that each of them would sell his share of the collar for this thing, and for nought else—that she should lie a night by each of them: wherefore, whether she liked it better or worse, on such wise did she strike the bargain with them; and so the four nights being outworn, and all conditions fulfilled, they delivered the collar to Freyia; and she went home to her bower, and held her peace hereof, as if nought had befallen.

Chapter II. Of the Stealing of Freyia's Collar, and How She May Have It Again

There was a man called Farbauti, which carl had to wife a carline called Laufey; she was both slim and slender, therefore was she called Needle. One child had these, a son called Loki; nought great of growth was he, but betimes shameless of tongue and nimble in gait; over all men had he that craft which is called cunning; guileful was he from his youth up, therefore was he called Loki the Sly.

He betook himself to Odin at Asgard and became his man. Ever had Odin a good word for him, whatsoever he turned to; yet withal he oft laid heavy labours upon him, which forsooth he turned out of hand better than any man looked for: moreover, he knew wellnigh all things that befell, and told all he knew to Odin.

So tells the tale that Loki knew how that Freyia had gotten the collar, yea and what she had given for it; so he told Odin thereof, and when Odin heard of it he bade Loki get the collar and bring it to him. Loki said it was not a likely business, because no man might come into Freyia's bower without the will of her; but Odin bade him go his ways and not come back before he had gotten the collar. Then Loki turned away howling, and most of men were glad thereof whenas Loki throve nought.

But Loki went to Freyia's bower, and it was locked; he strove to come in, and might not; and cold it was without, so that he fast began to grow a-cold.

So he turned himself into a fly, and fluttered about all the locks and the joints, and found no hole therein whereby he might come in, till up by the gable-top he found a hole, yet no bigger than one might thrust a needle through; none the less he wriggled in thereby. So when he was come in he peered all about to see if any waked, but soon he got to see that all were asleep in the bower. Then in he goeth unto Freyia's bed, and sees that she hath the collar on her with the clasp turned downward. Thereon Loki changed himself into a flea, and sat on Freyia's cheek, and stung her so that she woke and turned about, and then fell asleep again. Then Loki drew from off him his flea's shape, and undid the collar, and opened the bower, and gat him gone to Odin therewith.

Next morn awoke Freyia and saw that the doors were open, yet unbroken, and that the goodly collar was gone. She deemed she knew what guile had wrought it, so she goeth into the hall when she is clad, and cometh before Odin the king, and speaketh to him of the evil he has let be wrought against her in the stealing of that dear thing, and biddeth him give her back her jewel.

Odin says that in such wise hath she gotten it, that never again shall she have it. 'Unless forsooth thou bring to pass, that two kings, each served of twenty kings, fall to strife, and fight under such weird and spell, that they no sooner fall adown than they stand up again and fight on: always unless some christened man be so bold of heart, and the fate and fortune of his lord be so great, that he shall dare go into that battle, and smite with weapons these men: and so first shall their toil come to an end, to whatsoever lord it shall befall to loose them from the pine and trouble of their fell deeds.'

Hereto said Freyia yea, and gat her collar again.

Chapter III. Of King Erling, & Sorli his Son

In those days, when four-and-twenty winters were worn away from the death of Peace-Frodi, a king ruled over the Uplands in Norway called Erling. He had a queen and two sons; Sorli the Strong the elder, and Erlend the younger: hopeful were they both, but Sorli was the stronger. They fell to warfare so soon as they were of age thereto; they fought with the viking Sindri, son of Sveigr, the son of Haki, the sea-king, at the Elfskerries; and there fell the viking Sindri and all his folk; there also fell Erlend Erlingson. Thereafter Sorli sailed into the East-salt-sea, and harried there, and did so many doughty deeds that late it were ere all were written down.

Chapter IV. Sorli Slayeth King Halfdan

There was a king hight Halfdan, who ruled over Denmark, and abode in a stead called Roi's-well; he had to wife Hvedna the Old, and their sons were Hogni and Hakon, men peerless of growth and might, and all prowess: they betook them to warfare so soon as they were come to man's estate.

Now cometh the tale on Sorli again, for on an autumn-tide he sailed to Denmark. King Halfdan was minded as at this time to go to an assembly of the kings; he was well stricken in years when these things betid. He had a dragon so good that never was such another ship in all Norway for strength's sake, and all craftsmanship. Now was this ship lying moored in the haven, but King Halfdan was a-land and had let brew his farewell drink. But when Sorli saw the dragon, so great covetise ran into his heart that he must needs have her: and forsooth, as most men say, no ship so goodly hath ever been in the Northlands, but it were the dragon Ellida, or Gnod, or the Long Worm.

So Sorli spake to his men, bidding them array them for battle; 'for we will slay King Halfdan and have away his dragon.'

Then answered his word a man called Sævar, his Forecastle-man and Marshal: 'Ill rede, lord,' saith he; 'for King Halfdan is a mighty lord of great renown, and hath two sons to avenge him, who are either of them full famous men.'

'Let them be mightier than the very Gods,' said Sorli, 'yet shall I none the less join battle.'

So they arrayed them for the fight.

Now came tidings hereof to King Halfdan, and he started up and fared down to the ships with all his men, and they got them ready for battle.

Some men set before King Halfdan that it was ill rede to fight, and it were best to flee away because of the odds; but the king said that they should fall everyone across the other's feet or ever he should flee. So either side arrayed them, and joined battle of the fiercest; the end whereof was such that King Halfdan fell and all his folk, and Sorli took his dragon and all that was of worth.

Thereafter heard Sorli, that Hogni was come from warfare, and lay by Odins-isle; so thitherward straight stood Sorli, and when they met he told him of the fall of Halfdan his father, and offered him atonement and self-doom, and they to become foster-brethren. But Hogni gainsayed him utterly: so they fought as it sayeth in Sorli's Song. Hakon went forth full fairly, and slew Sævar, Sorli's Banner-bearer and Forecastle-man, and therewith Sorli slew Hakon, and Hogni slew Erling the king, Sorli's father.

Then they fought together, Hogni and Sorli, and Sorli fell before Hogni for wounds and weariness' sake: but Hogni let heal him, and they swore the oath of brotherhood thereafter, and held it well whiles they both lived. Sorli was the shortest-lived of them; he fell in the East-sea before the vikings, as it saith in the Sorli-Song, and here saith:

> Fell there the fight-greedy,
> Foremost of war-host,
> Eager in East-seas,
> All on Hells' hall-floor;
> Died there the doughty
> In dale-fishes joy-tide,
> With byrny-rod biting
> The vikings in brand-thing.

But when Hogni heard of the fall of Sorli, he went a-warring in the East-lands that same summer, and had the victory in every place, and became king thereover; and so say men that twenty kings paid tribute to King Hogni, and held their realms of him.

Hogni won so great fame from his doughty deeds and his warfare that he was as well known by name north in the Finn-steads, as right away in Paris-town; yea, and all betwixt and between.

Chapter V. Hedinn Heareth Tell of King Hogni, and Cometh to the North-Lands

Hiarandi was the name of a king who ruled over Serkland; a queen he had, and one son named Hedinn, who from his youth up was peerless of growth, and strength, and prowess: from his early days he betook him to warfare, and became a Sea-king, and harried wide about Spain and the land of the Greeks, and all realms thereabout, till twenty kings paid tribute to him, and held of him land and fief.

The Tale of Hogni and Hedinn

On a winter abode Hedinn at home in Serkland, and it is said that on a time he went into the wood with his household; and so it befell him to be alone of his men in a certain wood-lawn, and there in the wood-lawn he saw a woman sitting on a chair, great of growth and goodly of aspect: he asked her of her name, and she named herself Gondul.

Then fell they a-talking, and she asked him of his doughty deeds, and lightly he told her all, and asked her if she wotted of any king who was his peer in daring and hardihood, in fame and furtherance; and she said she wotted of one who fell nowise short of him, and who was served of twenty kings no less than he, and that his name was Hogni, and his dwelling north in Denmark.

'Then wot I,' said Hedinn, 'that we shall try it which of us twain is foremost.'

'Now will it be time for thee to go to thy men,' said Gondul; 'they will be seeking thee.'

So they departed and he fared to his men, but she was left sitting there.

But so soon as spring was come Hedinn arrayed his departure, and had a dragon and three hundred men thereon: he made for the Northlands, and sailed all that summer and winter, and came to Denmark in the Springtide.

Chapter VI. Hogni and Hedinn Meet, and Swear Brotherhood to Each Other

King Hogni sat at home this while, and when he heard tell how a noble king is come to his land he bade him home to a glorious feast, and that Hedinn took. And as they sat at the drink, Hogni asked what errand Hedinn had thither, that had driven him so far north in the world. Hedinn said that this was his errand, that they twain should try their hardihood and daring, their prowess and all their craftsmanship; and Hogni said he was all ready thereto.

So betimes on the morrow fared they to swimming and shooting at marks, and strove in tilting and fencing and all prowess; and in all skill were they so alike that none thought he could see betwixt them which was the foremost. Thereafter they swore themselves foster-brethren, and should halve all things between them.

Hedinn was young and unwedded, but Hogni was somewhat older, and he had to wife Hervor, daughter of Hiorvard, who was the son of Heidrek, who was the son of Wolfskin.

Hogni had a daughter, Hild by name, the fairest and wisest of all women, and he loved his daughter much. No other child had he.

Chapter VII. The Beguiling of Hedinn, and of his Evil Deed

The tale telleth that Hogni went a-warring a little hereafter, and left Hedinn behind to ward the realm. So on a day went Hedinn into the wood for his disport, and blithe was the weather. And yet again he turned away from his men and came into a certain wood-lawn, and there in the lawn beheld the same woman sitting in a chair, whom he had seen aforetime in Serkland, and him seemed that she was now gotten fairer than aforetime.

Yet again she first cast a word at him, and became kind in speech to him; she held a horn in her hand shut in with a lid, and the king's heart yearned toward her.

She bade the king drink, and he was thirsty, for he was gotten warm; so he took the horn and drank, and when he had drunk, lo a marvellous change came over him, for he remembered nought of all that was betid to him aforetime, and he sat him down and talked with her. She asked whether he had tried, as she had bidden him, the prowess of Hogni and his hardihood.

Hedinn said that sooth it was: 'For he fell short of me in nought in any mastery we tried: so now are we called equal.'

'Yet are ye nought equal,' said she.

'Whereby makest thou that?' said he.

'In this wise,' said she; 'that Hogni hath a queen of high kindred, but thou hast no wife.'

He answers: 'Hogni will give me Hild, his daughter, so soon as I ask her; and then am I no worse wedded than he.'

'Minished were thy glory then,' she said, 'wert thou to crave Hogni of alliance. Better were it, if forsooth thou lack neither hardihood nor daring according to thy boast, that thou have away Hild, and slay the queen in this wise: to wit, to lay her down before the beak of that dragon-ship, and let smite her asunder therewith in the launching of it.'

Now so was Hedinn ensnared by evil heart and forgetfulness, because of the drink he had drunken, that nought seemed good to him save this; and he clean forgat that he and Hogni were foster-brethren.

So they departed, and Hedinn fared to his men; and this befell when summer was far spent.

Now Hedinn ordained his men for the arraying of the dragon, saying that he would away for Serkland. Then went he to the bower, and took Hild and the queen, one by either hand, and went forth with them; and his men took Hild's raiment and fair things. Those men only were in the realm, who durst do nought for Hedinn and his men; for full fearful of countenance was he.

But Hild asked Hedinn what he would, and he told her; and she bade him do it not: 'For,' quoth she, 'my father will give me to thee if thou woo me of him.'

'I will not do so much as to woo thee,' said Hedinn.

'And though,' said she, 'thou wilt do no otherwise than bear me away, yet may my father be appeased thereof: but if thou do this evil deed and unmanly, doing my mother to death, then never may my father be appeased: and this wise have my dreams pointed, that ye shall fight and lay each other a-low; and then shall yet heavier things fall upon you: and great sorrow shall it be to me, if such a fate must fall upon my father that he must bear a dreadful weird and heavy spells: nor have I any joy to see thee sorehearted under bitter toil.'

Hedinn said he heeded nought what should come after, and that he would do his deed none the less.

'Yea, thou mayest none other do,' said Hild, 'for not of thyself dost thou it.'

Then went Hedinn down to the strand, and the dragon was thrust forth, and the queen laid down before the beak thereof; and there she lost her life.

So went Hedinn aboard the dragon: but when all was dight he would fain go a-land alone of his men, and into the self-same wood wherein he had gone aforetime: and so, when he was come into the wood-lawn, there saw he Gondul sitting in a chair: they greeted each the other friendly, and then Hedinn told her of his deeds, and thereof was she well content. She had with her the horn whereof he had drunk afore, and again she bade him drink thereof; so he took it and drank, and when he had drunk sleep came upon him, and he fell tottering into her lap: but when he slept she drew away from his head and spake: 'Now hallow I thee, and give thee to lie under all those spells and the weird that Odin commanded, thee and Hogni, and all the hosts of you.'

Then awoke Hedinn, and saw the ghostly shadow of Gondul, and him-seemed she was waxen black and over big; and all things came to his mind again, and mighty woe he deemed it. And now was he minded to get him far away some-whither, lest he hear daily the blame & shame of his evil deed.

So he went to the ship and they unmoored speedily: the wind blew off shore, and so he sailed away with Hild.

Chapter VIII. The Weird Falleth on These Twain, Hogni and Hedinn

Now cometh Hogni home, and comes to wot the sooth, that Hedinn hath sailed away with Hild and the dragon Halfdans-loom, and his queen is left dead there. Full wroth was Hogni thereat, and bade men turn about straightway and sail after Hedinn. Even so did they speedily, and they had a wind of the best, and ever came at eve to the haven whence Hedinn had sailed the morning afore.

But on a day whenas Hogni made the haven, lo the sails of Hedinn in sight on the main; so Hogni, he and his, stood after them; and most sooth is it told that a head-wind fell on Hedinn, whiles the same fair wind went with Hogni.

So Hedinn brought-to at an isle called Ha, and lay in the roadstead there, and speedily came Hogni up with him; and when they met Hedinn greeted him softly: 'Needs must I say, foster-brother,' saith he, 'how evil hath befallen me, that none may amend save thou: for I have taken from thee thy daughter and thy dragon; and thy queen I have done to death. And yet is this deed done not from my evil heart alone, but rather from wicked witchcraft and evil spells; and now will I that thou alone shear and shape betwixt us. But I will offer thee to forego both Hild and the dragon, my men and all my wealth, and to fare so far out in the world that I may never come into the Northlands again, or thine eyesight, whiles I live.'

Hogni answered: 'I would have given thee Hild, hadst thou wooed her; yea, and though thou hadst borne away Hild from me, yet for all that might we have had peace: but whereas thou hast now wrought a dastard's deed in the laying down of my queen and slaying of her, there is no hope that I may ever take atonement from thee; but here, in this place, shall we try straightway which of us twain hath more skill in the smiting of strokes.'

Hedinn answered: 'Rede it were, since thou wilt nought else but battle, that we twain try it alone, for no man here is guilty against thee saving I alone: and nowise meet it is that guiltless men should pay for my folly and ill-doing.'

But the followers of either of them answered as with one mouth, that they would all fall one upon the other rather than that they two should play alone.

So when Hedinn saw that Hogni would nought else but battle, he bade his men go up a-land: 'For I will fail Hogni no longer, nor beg off the battle: so let each do according to his manhood.'

So they go up a-land now and fight: full fierce is Hogni, and Hedinn apt at arms and mighty of stroke.

Soothly is it said that such mighty and evil spells went with the weird of these, that though they clave each other down to the shoulders, yet still they stood upon their feet and fought on: and ever sat Hild in a grove and looked on the play.

So this travail and torment went on ever from the time they first fell a-fighting till the time that Olaf Tryggvison was king in Norway; and men say that it was an hundred and forty and three years before the noble man, King Olaf, brought it so about that his courtman loosed them from this woeful labour and miserable grief of heart.

Chapter IX. Hogni & Hedinn are Loosed from their Weird

So tells the tale, that in the first year of the reign of King Olaf he came to the Isle of Ha, and lay in the haven there on an eve. Now such was the way of things in that isle, that every night whoso watched there vanished away, so that none knew what was become of them.

On this night had Ivar Gleam-bright to hold ward: so when all on shipboard were asleep Ivar took his sword, which Iron-shield of Heathwood had owned erst, and Thorstein his son had given to Ivar, and all his war-gear he took withal, and so went up on to the isle.

But when he was gotten up there, lo a man coming to meet him, great of growth, and all bloody, and exceeding sorrowful of countenance. Ivar asked that man of his name; and he said he was called Hedinn, the son of Hiarandi, of the blood of Serkland.

'Sooth have I to tell thee,' said he, 'that whereas the watchmen have vanished away, ye must lay it to me and to Hogni, the son of Halfdan; for we and our men are fallen under such sore weird and labour, that we fight on both night and day; and so hath it been with us for many generations of men; and Hild, the daughter of Hogni, sitteth by and looketh on. Odin hath laid this weird upon us, nor shall aught loose us therefrom till a christened man fight with us; and then whoso he smiteth down shall rise up no more; and in such wise shall each one of us be loosed from his labour. Now will I crave of thee to go with me to the battle, for I wot that thou art well christened; and thy king also whom thou servest is of great goodhap, of whom my heart telleth me, that of him and his men shall we have somewhat good.'

Ivar said yea to going with him; and glad was Hedinn thereat, and said: 'Be thou ware not to meet Hogni face to face, and again that thou slay not me before him; for no mortal man may look Hogni in the face, or slay him if I be dead first: for he hath the Ægis-helm in the eyes of him, nor may any shield him thence. So there is but one thing for it, that I face him and fight with him, whiles thou goest at his back and so givest him his death-blow; for it will be but easy work for thee to slay me, though I be left alive the longest of us all.'

Therewith went they to the battle, and Ivar seeth that all is sooth that Hedinn hath told him: so he goeth to the back of Hogni, and smiteth him into his head, and cleaveth him down to the shoulders: and Hogni fell dead, and never rose up again.

Then slew Ivar all those men who were at the battle, and Hedinn last of all, and that was no hard work for him. But when he came to the grove wherein Hild was wont to sit, lo she was vanished away.

Then went Ivar to the ship, when it was now daybreak, and he came to the king and told him hereof: and the king made much of his deed, and said that it had gone luckily with him.

But the next day they went a-land, and thither where the battle had been, and saw nowhere any signs of what had befallen there: but blood was seen on Ivar's sword as a token thereof; and never after did the watchman vanish away.

So after these things the king went back to his realm.

The End of this Tale.

THE SAGA OF ÁSMUNDR, KILLER OF CHAMPIONS

TRANSLATED BY ALISON FINLAY

Introduction

Ásmundar saga kappabana is a short *fornaldarsaga* that tells of a fight to the death between two half-brothers. It is preserved in two manuscripts: Cod. Holm. 7 4to of the early fourteenth century, and in part in the fifteenth-century AM 586 4to (a fragmentary version that, although more expansive, covers only chapters 5–7 of the saga). It was probably written in the late thirteenth century, but a large part of its interest lies in the two concluding poems in *fornyrðislag,* spoken by the two protagonists, from which the saga appears to derive most of its material.

The saga has attracted considerable attention, largely from German scholars, because of its apparent relationship with the so-called Hildebrand legend, the subject of the oldest Germanic lay—and indeed, the only one to survive in Old High German—the *Hildebrandslied*. This now fragmentary poem, written probably *c*.800, consists of 68 lines of alliterative verse identical in form to that of Old English poetry:

> Ik gihorta ðat seggen
> ðat sih urhettun   ænon muotin
> Hiltibrant enti Haðubrant   untar heriun tuem
> sunufatarungo   iro saro rihtun
> garutun se iro guðhamun   gurtun sih iro suert ana
> helidos ubar hringa   do sie to dero hiltiu ritun.

> I heard tell
> That warriors met   in single combat
> Hildebrand and Hadubrand   between two armies
> son and father   prepared their armour
> made ready their battle garments   girded on their swords
> the warriors, over their ring mail   when they rode to battle.

The poem relates the meeting of two warriors, apparently acting as 'champions' for two opposing armies. The elder, Hildebrand, asks about the antecedents of his younger opponent, Hadubrand, who reveals himself as Hildebrand's own son, left behind as a child when Hildebrand fled the tyranny of Odoacer to take service with Theodoric. Hildebrand responds enigmatically that the young man will never fight a closer kinsman (thus indirectly acknowledging his paternity), but the young man is belligerent, refuses the offer of gifts and accuses his opponent of deception, since he believes his father has died. The poem breaks off as the duel gets under way, but Hildebrand's own words suggest that one of the two must kill the other. The nature of the ending is largely guesswork, such as that outlined by Gummere in the introduction to his translation (Gummere 1923, 173):

> The original . . . must have had a tragic ending; the theme demands it, and not only a scrap of this same tale in Old Norse, but analogy of other cases, sustains the demand. The father unwillingly kills his son. Such things must have actually happened now and again in the days of the *comitatus* . . . but the killing of near kin remained the capital crime for a German . . . Loyalty to one's lord was a Germanic virtue which grew stronger with the necessities of constant warfare, until it came to be supreme, and thus overshadowed the obligations of actual kindred. Hildebrand is a victim of the clash of these two duties,—and not for once only. Thirty years before this crowning tragedy, he was forced to choose between his lord, a banished man, and his wife and child. Now the child faces him in arms.

The 'scrap of this same tale in Old Norse' referred to by Gummere is in fact the reference, in the poem spoken by Hildibrandr at the end of *Ásmundar saga*, to his unwilling slaying of his own son. This is replicated in the saga prose by Hildibrandr's arbitrary killing of his son (who is not otherwise mentioned in the saga prose), under the influence of berserk rage, as he goes out to meet Ásmundr in battle. The saga author tried to incorporate in his text all the material provided by the verses, but clearly had no more idea how this element related to the story alluded to by the Norse verses—a battle between half-brothers—than does the modern reader.

In his study of the sources of *Ásmundar saga*, E. F. Halvorsen argued convincingly that the saga author, while probably borrowing motifs and stylistic features from other *fornaldarsögur*, derived all his knowledge of the Hildebrand material from the verses cited in the saga. Halvorsen was not able to ascribe an origin or a date of composition to the verses themselves, but speculated that they might once have made part of a collection of poems such as those included in the extant manuscripts of Eddic poems—perhaps accompanied by a short prose preamble such as that found, for example, in *Vǫlundarkviða* (Halvorsen 1951, 52).

A version of these verses was also known to Saxo Grammaticus, who included his own elaboration of the story in Book VII of his *Gesta Danorum*. Like the author of *Ásmundar saga*, Saxo works backwards from the verses themselves to create his prose legend, citing his Latin adaptations of the verses to mark the end and climax. As with his adaptations of Norse verse elsewhere, Saxo 'does not only translate the old lays, he also desires to give them a correct Latin form, therefore he had to elaborate the abrupt Norse poems and give them a suitable beginning and end' (Halvorsen 1951, 17). Thus his equivalent to what is often called 'Hildibrandr's Death Song' (pp. 137–38 below) begins, in Peter Fisher's translation (Ellis Davidson and Fisher, I 223):

> I should like the hour to roll by in conversation;
> stop the sword-play, rest on the ground a little,
> vary the interval with talk and warm our hearts.
> Time remains for our purpose. Different destinies
> control our twin fates; death's lottery brings
> one to his appointed hour, while processions and glory
> and a chance to live the days of better years
> await the other. The omens distinguish us
> in separate roles. Danish territory bore you,
> Sweden me. Once Drot's maternal breast
> swelled for you; I too sucked milk from her teat.

While the generalising first eight lines do not correspond closely to the Old Norse poem, the final three accurately represent the second half of the first stanza:

> Drótt bore you
> in Denmark,
> and myself
> among the Swedes.

The form 'Drot' used by Saxo corresponds to the unusual name 'Drótt' used in the Norse of the brothers' mother. The author of *Ásmundar saga* evidently took this for a poetic *heiti* for a woman rather than a name, and replaced it in his prose version with 'Hildr', conventional in the *fornaldarsögur*.

Saxo again relies closely on his poetic source in detailing the assaults of Haldan (the figure corresponding to Ásmundr in his version) on the champions (Ellis Davidson and Fisher, I 224):

> I subdued in battle
> one alone, then two,
> three and four, and soon
> five followed by six,
> seven, eight together,
> then eleven single-handed.

This corresponds closely to the verse in the poem spoken by Ásmundr:

> Alone I fought one,
> and indeed two,
> five and four
> friends of the hall,
> on the field six and seven
> at the same time,
> I alone against eight,
> yet still I live.

Clearly the poems known to Saxo, writing late in the twelfth century, were very close to those quoted in *Ásmundar saga*, and probably derived from a common source. The points in common between Saxo's prose version and the saga can be listed in Halvorsen's summary (9–10):

1. The two swords; Saxo mentions them, and even gives them names, but he does not know that they were made by dwarfs.

2. Hildr-Drota is married twice.

3. Haldanus-Ásmundr fights with his half-brother to win a princess; the circumstances are different in the two sources.

4. Only Hildigerus-Hildibrandr knows that they are brothers.

5. The fight with the berserks.

6. The Death Song, and the death of Hildigerus-Hildibrandr.

7. The return of Haldanus-Ásmundr, and the second song.

Saxo's knowledge of essentially the same story as is recorded in the verses on which *Ásmundar saga* is based makes it certain that some version of the Hildibrandr story was circulating in Scandinavia in the twelfth century; in Halvorsen's view, this took the form of an oral saga, since the more extended poems postulated by other critics 'have disappeared completely' (1951, 10). He suggests that the oral story was known to the scribe who first recorded the verses, but lost by the time these were used by the saga author, who had no other direct source for his version of the tale. In truth, however, we have no indication other than the saga's verses for the form in which this material was transmitted to the north. Versions of the Hildebrand legend are also found in the thirteenth-century *Þiðreks saga* and in a Faroese ballad, *Snjólvskvæði*, 'possibly derived from a much changed version of the *Ásmundar saga*' (Halvorsen 1951, 50).

The little literary analysis that the saga has attracted has not yielded complimentary results. According to Halvorsen it is 'rather complicated and confused', the work of a 'mediocre' author (7; 27); he points to inconsistencies such as the curse placed by its maker on the fatal sword, that 'it will cause the death of the most noble brothers, [King Buðli's] daughter's sons', when in fact the sword only accounts for the death of one of the two, Hildibrandr; and to characters arbitrarily introduced and then summarily dismissed from the narrative when they have served their limited purpose. Ciklamini gives a more positive account of the saga's construction as 'a tale related with dexterous clarity and artlessness' (277), locating mediocrity rather in its audience as she discusses its 'adaptation to the taste of an undemanding peasant audience' (270). There is in fact a clear sense of structure in the saga's purposeful progress to its inevitable conclusion. The motif of the twin swords, products of the one forge as the brothers are products of the one womb, prefigures the unacknowledged kinship between the two, as when the messenger Vöggr remarks on the likeness not only between the men, but also between their weapons:

> I have never seen a third man as impressive as you and Hildibrandr are. He is fairer, but you are no less hardy . . . the weapons match the appearance of those who own them. The other is brighter and better made, but it is no sharper.

The repeated comments on the similarity between the brothers, rather than being a clumsy superfluity as Halvorsen suggests, reinforce the theme of the inevitability of the coming conflict. And there is some subtlety in the saga's treatment of Hildibrandr's reluctance to fight one who, he is coming to suspect, may be his half-brother. The author remains largely untouched by the tragic dilemma of the hero trapped between the demands of heroism and the obligations of kinship, but controls the inevitability and suspense of his intricate narrative.

The text translated here is that of the Stockholm manuscript, according to Detter's edition (that of the more widely available Guðni Jónsson edition is similar, but with different chapter divisions). The text of the verses is corrupt and difficult to interpret in places, although their general sense is clear. In producing the translation of the verses offered below, Detter's edition has been supplemented by that of Finnur Jónsson, and the commentary provided by Halvorsen (11–20), who relies on the edition by Heusler and Ranisch in *Eddica Minora*. Both editions make some emendations to the text, but these have not been recorded or commented upon here.

Bibliography

Ásmundar saga kappabana. In *Fornaldar sögur norðurlanda* 1954. 4 vols. Ed. Guðni Jónsson, I 383–408.

Ciklamini, M. 1966. 'The Combat between Two Half-Brothers: A Literary Study of the Motif in *Ásmundar saga kappabana* and *Saxonis Gesta Danorum*'. *Neophilologus* 50, 269–79, 70–79.

Detter, F., ed., 1891. *Zwei Fornaldarsögur: Hrólfssaga Gautrekssonar und Ásmundarsaga kappabana; nach Cod. Holm. 7, 4to*.

Ellis Davidson, Hilda, ed., and Peter Fisher, trans., 1979–80. *Saxo Grammaticus. The History of the Danes, Books I–IX*.

Finnur Jónsson, ed., 1912–15. 'Af Ásmundar saga kappabana'. In *Den norsk-islandske skjaldedigtning*. AII 320–22, BII 340–42.

Gummere, F., trans., 1923. *The Oldest English Epic: Beowulf, Finnsburg, Waldere, Deor, Widsith, and the German Hildebrand, Translated in the Original Metres with Introduction and and Notes,* 171–77.

Halvorsen, E. F. 1951. *On the Sources of the Ásmundarsaga kappabana*. Studia Norvegica 5.

Heusler, A. and W. Ranisch, eds, 1903. *Eddica Minora. Dichtungen eddischer Art aus den Fornaldarsögur und anderen Prosawerken*.

The Saga of Ásmundr, Killer of Champions

Chapter 1. Here begins the saga of Ásmundr, who is called 'Killer of Champions'

There was a king who is named as Buðli. He ruled over Sweden, powerful and splendid. It was his custom to favour greatly the most skilful craftsmen he could find, who made treasures for him. He had a queen, and a daughter who was called Hildr. It happened there that the queen died, and the king was without a wife.

It is said that one evening two men came to the king and went before him with their greetings. The king asked who they were, and one gave his name as Olíus, the other as Alíus,—'and we would like to receive lodging here for the winter.'

He asked if they were craftsmen of any kind, or equipped with skills. They declared they could skilfully make any object which required craftsmanship. The king directed them to a seat and bade them stay there.

At that time there were people visiting the king, and in the evening the king's craftsmen came into the hall and showed him artefacts, gold and weapons. They always did this, if people came there, to enhance the king's fame. Everyone praised this workmanship apart from the newcomers. They said little about it. There was one knife among the objects, elaborately worked. The king was told this, and he said that he thought they would not be able to make anything better.

He called them to him and said, 'Why are you so reluctant to praise the craftsmanship that is on display here? Can you do any better?'

They told the king that he could prove, if he liked, that this workmanship was worth little compared with theirs.

The king told them to make an object that was of excellent value—'if you don't want to show yourselves to be impostors.'

They said they would quickly prove that this workmanship was worthless and of poor quality. They drove the knife into the edge of the table in front of the king, and the blade immediately bent. Then they told the king to take his precious object, but said that they would try to make another knife. The king told them to do so, and then they made a knife and brought it to the king. He drew it across his beard, and it took off the beard and the skin, and came to rest in the flesh.

The king said, 'It must be true that you are skilled men, and now you must make me a gold ring,' and they did so, and brought it to the king.

He looked at it and said, 'It is true to say that I have never seen a ring that is a greater treasure.' And all those who saw it said the same.

The king declared that such men were servants of noble people, and then he said, 'Now you must make me two swords, which will surpass other workmanship no less than this handiwork of yours, and which will never strike a blow that does not cut.'

Olíus said that he was not willing to do this, and that he thought it not unlikely that it would be a serious matter if they were forced to do it, and said it was best to behave with moderation. The king said they must do it, whether reluctantly or not.

Then they got to work and made two swords, one each, and then went before the king and showed him the swords. The king looked at them, and they looked fine to him, 'but what qualities do they have?'

Olíus spoke; he said that he would not be able to strike a blow with that one that did not cut,—'And I think there will not be any flaws in it.'

The king said, 'It is good then, and we must test how well it has been tempered,' and he thrust the point into the upright of the high seat, and the sword bent a little, and then he bent it straight in a hole.

The craftsman said that was too harsh a test for the sword, and maintained that it was fit for blows, not for bending. The king said it would not withstand a blow if it failed in trials like this. And now he tried the sword that Alíus had made, and it sprang back straight as a splint, and in all ways it was finer than the other one, and it stood up to both the trials that the king made.

The king said, 'This one that Alíus made is even better, although both are good, and what are its qualities?'

Alíus said, 'This, lord: if they strike each other in the air when they are carried against each other, my sword will prevail, and yet their qualities can be called one and the same.'

Then the king took the sword made by Olíus, and tried to break it, and then the sword broke off at the hilt. The king told him to make a better sword, and he went off, angry, to the smithy and made a sword and gave it to the king. He made all the same trials as on the first one, and this one passed them all.

The king said: 'Now you have done well, but are there no disadvantages to it?'

He said, 'The sword is a good weapon, and yet certain drawbacks will bring about a change of fortune, for it will cause the death of the most noble brothers, your daughter's sons.'

The king said, 'You prophesy like a wretch; now the death of brothers shall be caused, but not noble ones,' and he struck at him, but they had taken a hasty departure, following the lower path.[1]

The king said, 'These are great enemies, and we must strive to prevent the sword harming anyone.'

Then the king had a leaden case made for the sword and had it sunk in the great lake by Agnafit.[2]

Chapter II. A Marriage

There was a splendid king called Helgi. He was a great warrior. Helgi went with warships in search of King Buðli and sent him a message that he would be his ally, and said that he wanted to make his acquaintance and receive entertainment from him. The king responded favourably to this. King Helgi went ashore to the hall and got a good reception there. Hildibrandr was the name of King Helgi's father, who ruled over the land of the Huns.

Then King Helgi said, 'I will make known my wish to you by requesting a marriage with your daughter. I can see honour for both in this, for me in defence of your land, and power for you in exchange.'

King Buðli said, 'I will agree to your proposal if she is in agreement with us.'

And then the proposal was put to her, and she yielded to the wish of her father, and now the feast was augmented according to the custom of noble men, and King Helgi married King Buðli's daughter Hildr, and afterwards father- and son-in-law were of one mind, and King Buðli had great faith in King Helgi.

He and Hildr had a son who was called Hildibrandr, who was very promising, and as soon as he was grown, his father King Helgi said, 'Your foster-father shall be my father Hildibrandr the Great, in the land of the Huns, and then it will be very likely that your future will turn out as is most fitting.'

Then King Helgi sent the boy there. King Hildibrandr gave him a splendid welcome and declared that he expected that a hero would be brought up there. After that King Helgi went raiding, while King Buðli grew old governing his lands.

---

[1] That is, sinking into the earth. This identifies the mysterious smiths as dwarfs (as they are clearly said to be in the final verses).

[2] Lake Mälaren.

Chapter III. King Álfr Goes to War

There was a king called Álfr who ruled over Denmark. His daughter was called Æsa the Fair. She was widely famed in all lands for her beauty and skill in needlework. Áki was the name of a powerful warrior in Denmark. He was greatly favoured by the king, and King Álfr had great faith in him.

The king summoned him and said, 'I want to undertake raiding this summer, and take into my possession a land that has been lying unguarded, yet it would bring fame to gain it.'

The hero replied, 'Lord, where do you know of an available land?'

The king said, 'King Buðli is now overcome with old age, and I want to take control of his dominion.'

Áki said, 'I don't wish to hinder great ventures; as usual after daring deeds, you will be intending to reward your friends for their work.'

Then King Álfr and Áki made ready their force and raided in Sweden in the kingdom of King Buðli and committed great ravages there with killing and seizure of property. And when King Buðli heard this he summoned his own force together, and got only a small company, for the support of his son-in-law Helgi was far away, and yet he sustained the attack and was overpowered and died in that battle, and King Álfr took as booty his daughter and a great deal of property, and with that they went home.

Then Álfr said, 'Now it has come about for us that we have plenty of power and wealth, and for your support, Áki, I wish to marry Buðli's daughter Hildr to you, although she already has a husband.'

Áki said, 'What rewards could be more to my taste than this? And it seems to me none the worse that Helgi was married to her before.'

After that Áki proceeded to marry Hildr, and they had one son. He was called Ásmundr. He soon grew large and strong and went on Viking expeditions as soon as he could, and brought into submission a great force of warriors.

Chapter IV. The Death of King Álfr at the Hands of Hildibrandr Huns' Champion

Now is to be taken up the story of his brother Hildibrandr, son of King Helgi, but King Helgi had fallen in raiding. Hildibrandr took control of a great force and wandered far and wide with his troop. He was related by marriage to the king who was called Laszínus. He was one of the most powerful of kings. He made his way with words of friendship to his kinsman, and was well received there. He now began to be eager for action, as his support increased.

There were noble and high-born dukes in Saxland then. Hildibrandr Huns' Champion now went against them and said that he wished them to pay him such honour as he demanded, or they would, like others, face dire consequences. The dukes had a sister, and she was deep in their confidence, for she was the wisest of them. Then they had a private conversation to consider what course they must take.

She said it was wiser to offer him tribute than to do battle, — 'and it is wise to behave moderately, but to turn and resist when there is some support,' and said it would happen here as elsewhere that he would be victorious.

Then the dukes said that they were willing to grant him tribute. He said that was prudent, and they came to terms with that.

Hildibrandr Huns' Champion now subdued many peoples under him. Now he learned the news of the fall of his mother's father, King Buðli. He then summoned his force to him again and called a meeting.

He spoke, said it was known to men what difficulties there were with going on raids, and said that it was not fitting if one were to make raids on Vikings or others for little or no cause, while not avenging one's grandfather.

After that he moved his host into the kingdom of King Álfr, and said that the Danes had shown how to go about things. He made sparks fly and fires burn widely. King Álfr made a counter-attack with his host, and as soon as they met, they fought. Hildibrandr Huns' Champion had the nature of a berserk, and the berserk rage came over him. Duke Áki was not at this battle because he was away raiding.

Hildibrandr Huns' Champion went through King Álfr's battle formation, and it was bad to be in his way. He struck with both hands and, howling, attacked the royal standard, and in this battle fell King Álfr and a large part of his force, and after that the Huns went back. Hildibrandr then became most famous of all men, and always stayed at his estates in winter, and raided in summer.

Chapter V. Ásmundr's Expedition

Now the story is to be taken up where Ásmundr was raiding, and the Vikings considered him overbearing in assaults, and hardy. There was a man called Eyvindr *skinnhöll*,[3] of Danish descent, a handsome man,

---

[3] This nickname cannot be translated. Halvorsen (1951, 37) cites Magnus Olsen's suggestion that the correct reading is *skinnhæll* 'skin, leather heel', but this does not appear to help much.

powerful and wealthy and very prominent. And when Áki and his son Ásmundr came back from raiding, they were told the news of the death of King Álfr. They stayed quiet now. Ásmundr did not know of his close kinship with Hildibrandr, for his mother had told him nothing about it.

Eyvindr skinnhöll went to see Princess Æsa the Fair and said he wanted to propose marriage to her, said that his status and wealth, descent and success were known to her. She said she would abide by the advice of her friends in her answer.

After that she put the case to Áki and her foster-brother Ásmundr. Áki said he would not urge this. Then Ásmundr said, 'You must not marry Eyvindr. You must marry me.'

She said, 'Foster-brother, he has more authority in the country, and lives more grandly, but I think that you are more of a man.'

Ásmundr said, 'Give me your blessing, and then honour may come to both of us from this match.'

She said, 'I will marry that one of you,' she said, 'who brings me fairer hands from raiding in the autumn.'

Then they dropped this discussion, and they both went raiding as usual, and Ásmundr often risked great danger for large returns, and so gained in wealth and fame, while Eyvindr often stayed among the cooks and did not take his glove off his hand.

And when autumn came they both went to see the princess, each with his men. Eyvindr went forward first and asked the princess to look at his hands.

Æsa the Fair said, 'These hands have been well cared for, and are white and fair; they have not stained themselves in blood or grown ugly with gashes. Let me now see, Ásmundr, your hands,' she said.

He stretched out his hands, and they were scarred and rather dark with blood and cuts from weapons, and as he reached out of his clothing they were laden with gold rings up to the shoulders.

Then the princess said, 'Yet it is my decision that Ásmundr's hands are fairer altogether, and you, Eyvindr, are out of this match.'

Ásmundr said, 'Then I must be chosen, lady.'

She said, 'First you must avenge my father, for it befits me to marry only a man who takes this vengeance and wins fame against Hildibrandr Huns' Champion.'

Then said Ásmundr, 'How can he be defeated, when no one wins against him? What do you advise?'

She said, 'I have heard that a sword is hidden in the lake by Agnafit, and I have heard a report that if that sword were carried against the one that Hildibrandr has, his sword must fail. But near the lake lives an old peasant, my friend, and he will give you a conveyance at my request.'

Ásmundr said that it would show how eager he was to marry her if he agreed to take this risk.

After this Ásmundr went alone to the peasant and told him his business and gave him the princess's message. The peasant bade him welcome. He kept looking at Ásmundr during the evening.

Ásmundr said, 'Why are you looking at me?'

He said that there was a reason. Ásmundr said, 'How long have you lived here?'

He said he had lived there all his life,—'but what I am thinking about now is that messengers of King Buðli stayed here a long time ago; they were taking Hildibrandr to be fostered by King Hildibrandr, and you are the next most promising man I have seen after him, and most like him to look at.'

Ásmundr said, 'I don't know of any kinship between us; but what do you know of this sword, where it is hidden, which is said to be so excellent?'

He said, 'I was here when it was sunk, and I have marked exactly where it is hidden, and it will still be undamaged, in my opinion.'

Then said Ásmundr, 'Then take me there, according to the princess's message.'

He said he must do so. He took with him a big flitch of bacon and a log of firewood.

Ásmundr said, 'What is that for, farmer?'

He answered, 'You will be cold enough when you come up, even if you warm yourself next to this.'

Ásmundr said, 'You are very sensible.'

Then they went onto a boat, and when Ásmundr least expected it, the peasant said, 'Just here.'

Then Ásmundr jumped overboard and dived, and when he came up he wanted to go down a second time.

The peasant said, 'That won't do for you, warm yourself now and eat,' and he did so.

And the second time when he dived, he recognised the case, and lifted it a little and went up and warmed himself. And now he dived a third time, and he got hold of the case, and they carried it ashore, and then Ásmundr broke open the case with an axe, and the point broke off and stuck in the sword's blade.

Ásmundr said, 'You have served well, old man, and accept a gold ring from me for your work, and visit me as a friend if you need to.'

The old man thanked him, and they parted. After that Ásmundr went home and told the princess.

She said, 'Now much has been achieved, and you will be an excellent man. Now a plan is under way: I will send you to the dukes in Saxland who have lost their dominion to Hildibrandr, and to their sister, for she is a wise woman, and my advice is to deal then with such things as will befall, for I guess that most will stumble before you in the face of your onslaught and good provision of weapons.'

And then Ásmundr went away.

Chapter VI. The Discussion of the Dukes and their Sister with Ásmundr

Now it is to be told what happened in Saxland, that one day the dukes' sister began to speak: 'My dreams show me that an excellent man is to visit us here, who will bring us great good fortune and our dominion.'

The brothers welcomed this, and that evening they saw riding to the hall a large man with splendid weapons, and the dukes went to meet him and invited him to stay there. He said he would accept. They seated him between themselves, and their sister served them and then sat down to speak with him and her brothers.

She said then: 'We do not know much about your condition, but we can see that an air of greatness surrounds you, and we believe that some good will come to us from you and your coming here. Now, you will have heard what hardship we suffer under the oppression of Hildibrandr Huns' Champion. We first submitted to tribute, but now we must undergo challenges to duels from his berserks every season, and an estate must always be forfeited for each duel. Thus we have lost both our men and our estates, and now there are no more than twelve estates left in our dukedom.'

Ásmundr replied, 'Lady,' he said, 'you complain to me of a great injury, and it would be necessary to calm this storm; that is why I have come to defend your dominion, if I can.'

The dukes said that it would not be long before a duel would be demanded. Ásmundr replied, 'Then it must be answered.'

He stayed there now in good favour.

Chapter VII. About the Messenger

Now is to be told about King Laszínus and Hildibrandr Huns' Champion, his kinsman by marriage.

Hildibrandr said, 'Is the time not come when a duel is to be fought against the dukes and their men? It wouldn't be difficult now to get the estates that are left.'

The king said, 'Rather, we'll send a man to them and find out if they can be taken more easily.'

The man who was sent was called Vöggr. Nothing is said of his journey until he came to the dukes. He went into the hall and before the tables and then said, 'King Laszínus and the great Hildibrandr, Huns' Champion, wish to know whether you are willing to come to a duel, or give up what is left without a struggle.'

The dukes replied, 'Matters now stand so that if our possessions seem too great, it is of less account to lose them than good men.'

Ásmundr said, 'Why do you speak so? Is there not all the more need to hold on, the less is left?'

Vöggr looked at him. Ásmundr said, 'Why are you looking so fixedly at me?'

He said, 'It is because I have never seen a third man as impressive as you and Hildibrandr are. He is fairer, but you are no less hardy, and Hildibrandr has heard that an unknown man has come here with fine weapons, and I must see your sword.'

Ásmundr said it was for him to decide. He now looked at it and said, 'In this case the weapons match the appearance of those who own them. The other is brighter and better made, but it is no sharper.'

Ásmundr said he did not know that,—'but you will want to know what message to take.'

He said that was so. Ásmundr said, 'Tell your leaders that a man will come to the duel on behalf of the dukes.'

Now Vöggr rode home and greeted the king and Hildibrandr.

Hildibrandr said, 'What answer can you give about the dukes' decision?'

Vöggr answered, 'I expect they will not fail to come to the duel.'

Hildibrandr said, 'They are now being very tough, or else that is because of that unknown man; how did his appearance seem to you? You are discerning.'

Vöggr said, 'His bearing is such that he is well-mannered, very like you about the eyes, and it seemed likely to me that he would be very brave, and he has a sword more like the one you have than any I have ever seen, and I think that it has come from the same forge.'

Hildibrandr said, 'You are greatly impressed by this man. Don't you think that my sword will be equal to his sword, or will he be my equal?'

Vöggr replied, 'I do not know whether he is your equal. I do know that he who fights against him will be put to the test, for he is certainly a capable man.'

Hildibrandr said, 'You speak highly of him.' And now Hildibrandr had one of his warriors ride to the duelling ground.

And now Ásmundr was told, and he gave orders for his horse to be caught and his armour brought.

The dukes said, 'We offer you our troops.'

He said he must go alone into the fight. He now rode to where the duel was to take place, and now they rode at each other with drawn swords, and with the first stroke Ásmundr cut him in two in the middle, then flung the pieces out into the river, and then they drifted past the king's fortress.

Hildibrandr said, 'Our companion is taking a long time to dispatch this unknown man.'

Then one man said, 'Lord,' he said, 'now you have a chance to see him floating down the river, and he is in two pieces.'

He said, 'That is a sufficiently big blow, and now let two of our men put themselves forward against him and dispose of him the more quickly.'

They said that was no great deed. Hildibrandr said, 'It will be our gain if you win a swift victory over him.'

And the next day they rode to the battlefield, two against Ásmundr.

He said, 'The berserks here have an unusual rule, since two swords come against one, but I am quite prepared to take on the fight against the two of you.'

They thought it dishonourable for the two of them to stand before one, and both struck at him, but he drew his shield in front of him and struck each of them a death-blow. Then he rode back to the dukes, and they came towards him to greet him. He said he reckoned that three of the estates had been won back for them in his venture.

Then the dukes' sister said, 'Our dreams have not been astray about this man's coming.'

Now he stayed there in high honour and won great fame from this.

Hildibrandr was now told this, and he said, 'It seems to me no marvel for one man to vanquish two. Now four men shall be appointed to oppose him.'[4]

The champions said that it was obvious that they would take him apart in four places, and now they rode to the battleground with fine helmets and bright byrnies and keen swords. Now news of this came before Ásmundr and the dukes. Then they asked him to go with an equal number of men. He said he did not want to do that, said that it was usual to be opposed by one at a time, but that it would be well worthwhile if four estates were gained. And then they met.

---

[4] The close dependence of the saga account on the verses is shown by the fact that both enumerate the numbers opposing Ásmundr as one, two, then four, without inserting three. Saxo's version does include three.

Ásmundr said, 'It is obvious that you think yourselves worth little, since four of you put yourselves forward against one, and these cannot be called champions but rather infantrymen.'

They grew terribly angry at his words and attacked him at once, but the sword he carried cut byrnies and helmets as smoothly as tree-bark, and spared neither human bone nor flesh, and it was wielded by one who had a strong arm and a good heart. They got great wounds from him, and their encounter was short, and he killed the four of them and threw them out into the river with their horses.

Now Hildibrandr learned of this and said, 'Now either our men are less warlike than we thought, or else this man is a master.'

Then he called to him five of the fiercest champions, spoke and said they would not be overtaxed to defeat a single man. They said they meant to cut his conceit down to size and feed his carcass to the beasts. Then they went out.

But when Ásmundr heard this he said, 'Today I mean to earn my keep.'

They said they were afraid that he was taking too much on himself, but said they were obliged to reward him with all honour. Then they met and fought at once, and Ásmundr struck hard and often, and in the end he killed them all.

But when Hildibrandr heard this, he said, 'His hand takes long to tire, and it must soon happen that he will have succeeded in the fight.'

Then the hall hummed loudly with the bellowing of the berserks that this one man should have overcome so many.

Then Hildibrandr said, 'Now let six of our men make ready, and then you can win the glory of avenging our men.'

Then they went to the duel, and when Ásmundr heard this, he made ready quickly and said, 'I have a sword as fit to kill six men with as three.'

And then they met. Then the champions said that he must drop the sword and give himself up.

He said, 'That shall not be, with my shield unhewn. And you have plenty of need to avenge your men.'

Then they fought, and he attacked hard. He used the same skill in cutting with the sword's blade now as before, and although he was wounded, he did not abate the sword's blows and cut some of them apart at the waist, and it finished so that he killed them all and went back to the dukes. They had gained plenty of followers, since their dominion was steadily growing, and now in everyone's house there was talk of this champion.

And again this news came to Hildibrandr, and he said, 'The tally of our men is getting thin now; how many are left?'

'Lord,' they said, 'there are twenty-six left.'

Hildibrandr replied, 'It can be estimated from now on that this unknown man is to be counted among the great champions, and he picks off whoever is found to oppose him, but a further seven shall be sent who have been longest in my service.'

Then they made ready. Ásmundr was now told that there would be no chance to rest.

He said, 'A meal break will only have been earned if seven estates are gained.'

Then he went, and seven champions came against him. Then said Ásmundr, 'Why does Hildibrandr pour out his men but sit at home himself and make me fight small fry?'

They grew very angry at his words and said he would be in no danger of fighting against Hildibrandr. Then they fought, and however they came to blows he killed them all. Then he pushed them out into the river.

And when Hildibrandr heard that, he said, 'Now much more important events have happened than we can allow to be forgotten. Now eight berserks must oppose him, for none of us can live with this if it is not avenged.'

Then they howled a lot and bit pieces out of their shields. But Ásmundr was with the dukes, and the news came to him that there was a further chance to fight.

Then said the dukes' sister, 'The honour that we lost has now all come back, and with greater power than has been reported to us.'

Ásmundr said, 'We must risk it, for he will lure out the berserks, but there is no control over them, and it would be better that their dominion should be added to our power, since you were unjustly deprived.'

Then he rode against them, and as soon as they met they fought, and that was the longest meeting, but it ended with him killing them all.

But when Hildibrandr heard that, he fumed with rage and said, 'This man is so lucky that a host of men make no mark on him. Now the eleven who are left must go for him.'

And when Ásmundr heard that he was silent.

The dukes said, 'Now we will share our company with you, and you will be the leader, and then you will win; you will not fight alone against the dauntless courage of so many.'

Ásmundr did not reply, and evening came, and people had a meal and then went to sleep.

Ásmundr dreamed that women stood over him with weapons and said, 'What is it with your look of fear? You are meant to be the leader of others, but you are afraid of eleven men. We are your prophetic spirits, and it is our task to defend you against men who have quarrels with the dukes, and those whom you have striving against you.'

With that he sprang up and made ready, though most people tried to dissuade him. Then he rode against the champions, and they thought they had his fate in their clutches and said it was more fitting for him to annoy Hildibrandr than to die. He said he was not as deathly pale as those he had killed earlier, and said it was obvious that fame would come from opposing a number like eleven. Then they fought, and they crowded around him, but he was difficult to overcome, and weapons made little impression on him, while his sword cut everything that came in its way and that it reached, and it ended so that he dealt death to them all.

The dukes had accompanied him, and declared that his great deeds would never be forgotten, and people began to say that he would not turn aside even if Hildibrandr Huns' Champion came against him, the most glorious of all men at that time.

Chapter VIII. The Fall of Hildibrandr

And when Hildibrandr learned that his champions were killed, berserk rage came over him, and he set out on his way at once, and said, 'It must not be said that I risked my men in the field but did not dare to fight myself.'

And in the fury that had come upon him, as he set out on his way he saw his son and killed him at once. Then he drove up along the river Rhine to meet Ásmundr. He had a shield on which there were marks, as many as the men as he had killed. And when Ásmundr learned this, he made ready for the meeting with him.

And as soon as they met they fought, and most of the blows were big enough. And when they had fought with great fury for a long time, Hildibrandr gathered his strength and struck at Ásmundr with both hands and with all his might, and as the sword entered the helmet it broke apart below the hilt, and the blade went whining down into the river, and he was wounded with many wounds. Then he spoke these verses:

> It is hard to foresee
> how one must
> by another
> be borne to death.
> Drótt bore you
> in Denmark,
> and myself
> among the Swedes.

> Two blades there were
> for battle ready,
> left by Buðli;
> now broken is one.
> Thus had the dead
> dwarves crafted them
> as none before
> nor after has done.
>
> By my head the shield
> shattered stands,
> on it tallied
> ten times eight
> marks of those
> men I have killed.
>
> By my head my sweet
> son is lying,
> the heir I fathered
> to follow me;
> Not willingly
> I denied him life.
>
> I ask you, brother,
> just one boon,
> A single favour,
> Do not refuse!
> with your clothing
> cover me,
> as other slayers
> seldom do.
>
> Now I must lie
> of life bereft,
> downed by the sword
> that deepens wounds.

After that Hildibrandr Huns' Champion died, and Ásmundr gave him an honourable funeral and was then displeased with his own deed. Then he did not meet the dukes, but went to the estate owned by his mother and by Princess Æsa the Fair. Then a man had it in mind to ask to marry her.[5] Ásmundr recited, as he came to the doorway of the hall:

> I did not expect
> that judgement,
> that it would be said
> I could not win,

[5] This suitor is unidentified in the saga.

> when the Huns chose me
> as their champion
> eight times
> for the lord's domain.
>
> Alone I fought one,
> and indeed two,
> five and four
> friends of the hall,
> on the field six and seven
> at the same time,
> I alone against eight,
> yet still I live.
>
> Then hesitated
> the heart in my breast,
> when eleven men
> offered me battle,
> until in my sleep
> the spirits told me
> that I must wage
> that weapon-play.
>
> Then came the aged
> Hildibrandr
> Huns' Champion,
> he was no match for me;
> and I made my mark
> meanwhile on him,
> below the helmet,
> a harsh war-token.

After that people gave him a good welcome, and he was called Ásmundr Killer of Champions.

The princess begged him not to be angry with her although she had helped to bring this about, and said there was much to excuse her, but she said there was a strong spell on the weapons. And though he would have been angry with her, he remembered her love and he prepared for his wedding and married Æsa the Fair, and he killed the man who had asked to marry her, and that man is not named. Then Ásmundr Killer of Champions became a man whose name was famous far and wide, and that is the end of this saga.